REACHING OUT

THE FINANCIAL POWER OF NICHE MARKETING

DORIS BARRELL, CRB, CRS, GRI
MARK NASH

With an afterword, " Fair Housing Law in Practice"
by Marcia L. Russell, DREI

Dearborn™
Real Estate Education

While a great deal of care has been taken to provide accurate and current information, the ideas, suggestions, general principles, and conclusions presented in this text are subject to local, state, and federal laws and regulations, court cases, and any revisions of same. The reader is urged to consult legal counsel regarding any points of law. This publication should not be used as a substitute for competent legal advice.

President: Roy Lipner
Publisher and Director of Distance Learning: Evan M. Butterfield
Development Editor: Chris Oler
Production Coordinator: Daniel Frey
Typesetter: Ellen Gurak
Creative Director: Lucy Jenkins

Published by Dearborn™ Real Estate Education
a division of Dearborn Financial Publishing, Inc.®
30 South Wacker Drive
Chicago, IL 60606-7481
http://www.dearbornRE.com

Printed in the United States of America.

03 04 10 9 8 7 6 5 4 3 2 1

Library of Congress Cataloging-in-Publication Data
Barrell, Doris.
   Reaching out : the financial power of niche marketing /
   Doris Barrell, Mark Nash.
     p. cm.
   Includes bibliographical references and index.
   ISBN 0-7931-6114-2
   1. Real estate business. 2. Real property-Marketing.
   3. Market segmentation. I. Nash, Mark. II. Title.

HD1375.B285 2003
333.33'068'1–dc21   2003010812

Table of Contents

Introduction

Anyone who has ever been involved in marketing understands that the primary goal is always to sell more—whether marketing a product or a service provided for a fee. More consumers or more clients equal more success, regardless of what you are marketing. To achieve this, you need to have a better product or service than anyone else in the competing market. The question becomes how to make your product the very best or your services the most desirable.

Although this book is primarily directed at those involved in real estate, the concept of niche marketing can be applied to any business that involves prospective sales.

What exactly is a "niche" market? The dictionary defines *niche* as "a nook or a special corner." When we are referring to people, we see the nook or special corner as a group of people who have something shared in common. This commonality may be a shared culture or nationality, or a matter of age, work experience, or lifestyle. Exactly what makes this particular group a niche really does not matter. The bonding that derives from having similar interests is what holds the group together. The niche marketer must attempt to become as knowledgeable as possible about every aspect of the niche members' wants and needs.

Some real estate professionals may discover that they have already been working a niche market although they may not have called it that. In many cases, however, aggressive sales agents are basically "shotgunning" their efforts. Agents may generate a lot of advertising, possibly specialize in a geographic farm, and in general stress either the product—specific properties—or promotion of themselves. In neither case is the important role of the consumer taken into account. By reaching out to touch prospective consumers where they actually *are* rather than where you think they might be, your entire marketing focus is redirected.

We, the co-authors of this book, are both active real estate practitioners, although in two entirely different fields and in two different geographic areas. Mark Nash came to the real estate world from a background of consumer product marketing. He attributes part of his interest in cultural and ethnic diversity from the time he spent studying in Greece. He is now a very successful REALTOR® practicing in the Chicago area and has had tremendous success in developing and working his own niche market.

Doris Barrell comes from an education background and has carried her love for teaching over into real estate. After almost 20 years in active practice, both as a salesperson and office manager, she now devotes her time to teaching continuing education courses and writing publications on various real estate subjects. She teaches several courses that are a part of the National Association of REALTORS® (NAR) Graduate Realtor® Institute program and is a certified instructor for the NAR "At Home with Diversity" course. One of her favorite classes to teach is one she developed called "Working with Senior Clients." She has also prepared and presented classes on developing real estate skills for the emerging real estate market in Eastern Europe and Southeast Asia. Her hands-on experience with those from other nationalities and cultures has added greatly to her understanding of the importance of niche marketing.

A casual conversation between Mark and Doris about the importance of niche marketing led to the development of this book. Whether you are reading it in hopes of expanding your own real estate practice, looking for tips on niche marketing in general, or simply reading out of general curiosity, we hope that you will find something here that helps you develop and enlarge your own marketing ability. Each Chapter from Two through Eight ends with a special interactive feature called "Steps to Niche Marketing Success." For those of you who are serious about trying niche marketing, these steps should provide you with enough hands-on training to get you started.

Scattered throughout the book are "In Real Life" boxes. Some of these are written by one of us; others are by other real estate professionals actively pursuing a niche market in their own market area.

In *Reaching Out*, we share with you our ideas on how to select a niche group, build upon it, continue to reaffirm the members of the niche, and develop successful marketing programs that will appeal to your selected group. Once you have developed a solid base of satisfied clients who will be quick to recommend you to others, you have the foundation for a constantly growing real estate practice. Prospecting should never end, but selective prospecting to your niche market can provide you with the ability to overcome cyclical changes in the market, changes in the organization of your brokerage firm, and even the natural tendency to quit prospecting once you have reached a certain income level.

A sense of power is achieved once you feel that you have more control over your own financial destiny. Having a large client base that is loyal to you and respects your abilities will assure you of continuing referrals. This constant source of new business will provide you with the financial power of niche marketing!

1

Real Estate Practice

YESTERDAY, TODAY, AND TOMORROW

The practice of real estate has gone through several paradigm shifts in the past two decades. Real estate professionals have moved from the position of totally representing the seller to providing services to either a seller client or a buyer client. Their role has shifted from provider of information to provider of service. Also, emphasis has shifted from the property itself to the people who are involved in the transaction. In this Chapter we will look at some of the ways that the practice of buying and selling properties has changed over the past two decades and how these changes affect the concept of niche marketing. Do you recall the saying, "You can't know where you're going if you don't know where you've been?" Let's start with a look at where we've been.

1

■ OLD ASSUMPTIONS—NEW REALITIES

Thirty years ago someone who decided to go into the real estate business obtained the proper licensing from the state, rented a small office space, put in a few phone lines, brought in a handful of agents, and was ready to roll. Agent splits on commissions ranged around the 50 percent mark, and the cost of operating an office was fairly minimal. Owning and operating a real estate brokerage firm had great potential to be a very profitable business. Over the years, this picture has changed drastically. Due to heavy competition for top-producing agents, some brokers now pay from 80 percent to 90 percent of the gross commission to both attract and keep these high-visibility agents. Some companies even offer a 100 percent commission to the agents and charge them for "rent" of office space and materials. When this factor is coupled this with the tremendous increases in the costs of operating an office, there really is not much left for the broker. Today's offices must be fully computerized and have telephone systems with voice mail, intercom, call forwarding, and so on. The cost of advertising has sky-rocketed in most areas. Paper and other supplies cost more, furniture and equipment prices have gone up, fees for membership in the local Multiple Listing Service (MLS) system have increased, and office rents are higher than ever.

The cost of houses has also greatly increased, which means more direct dollars in each commission; however, many items listed in the expense column are based on a percentage of the sales price, so the result is still a rather feeble bottom line. During the slow market years of the early 1990s only a very small percentage of brokerage companies claimed to be making any profit at all. You certainly cannot make it up in volume when you are showing a 5 percent to 10 percent annual loss!

The '90s were also strongly affected by the "pac man" syndrome of large firms gobbling up the little ones. According to

Laurie Moore of Real Trends,© the number of brokerage firms in this country dropped from 150,000 in 1990 to only 88,000 in 2000. In larger cities brokerage firms gravitate in one of two directions; to becoming either a mega-firm with dozens of offices and hundreds of agents scattered throughout the area or a small mom-and-pop or boutique operation. Small shops consisting of one broker plus four or five agents may still be common in smaller towns, but even there the large franchise firms like Century-21 or ERA are becoming more prevalent. The economic boost to the real estate market in the first part of the 2000s has been the salvation of many firms, although some of the smaller ones are just trying to build up enough financial credibility to become attractive for a buyout by one of the large firms.

Another significant change is the trend toward agents doing more work in their own homes. Today most agents have a home desktop computer and perhaps a laptop as well to carry along on appointments. Using cell phones or message answering systems, agents can be in constant contact with their clients. Hand-held Palm Pilot systems can even provide direct access to the MLS. Thanks to present-day high technology, there is no longer a need for every agent to have a fully equipped desk in the office.

What does this mean for the future from the agent's viewpoint? All the more reason to develop a strong niche market. Having an expanded client base with a specific target group provides job security for individual agents no matter what changes may occur in their brokerage firm. A niche market relies on personal involvement and direct referrals. It does not rely on expensive media advertising. It does not require extensive office space and amenities. Therefore, it is more insulated from the traditional ups and downs of the real estate market in general.

■ SELLER REPRESENTATION

The unique aspects of niche marketing make it well suited for a growing trend throughout the real estate industry today: fee for service. Some firms now offer a menu of services that the client may choose from and pay for according to an established fee. At a listing appointment, the client might be presented with a menu of various items that may be individually priced or offered in a combined package (see figure on next page).

Another variation on the traditional commission based on sales price is to quote a lower percentage if the property sells within the first 30 days, and a higher percentage if it takes longer. Yet another variation is to charge a lower percentage for properties listed over a certain price, and a higher percentage for something in a lower price range. (The assumption here is that it takes an equal amount of time and effort on the part of the agent, regardless of the sales price). A third approach is to charge for service by the hour rather than for the service performed.

The flexibility provided by the fee-for-service or variable commission options is also well suited to niche marketing. Whether the clients are immigrants, seniors, first-time home-buyers, or any of the many other possibilities, these niche markets often require a more flexible approach than what agents have used traditionally.

■ BUYER REPRESENTATION

The idea that a client would hire and pay a real estate professional to assist in buying a property is not entirely new. Representation of the buyer has prevailed in the commercial market for many years. Starting in the early 1980s in California, the concept of buyer agency began to spread throughout the

MENU OF SERVICES OFFERED BY ABC REALTY

- Entry into the MLS system

- Preparation of information brochure on the property

- Installation of For Sale sign and lockbox

- Hold open house for the public

- Hold broker open house for area brokers

- Advertise in city newspaper (price per entry)

- Advertise in local area newspaper (price per entry)

- Advertise on Cable TV Real Estate Channel (cost per entry)

- Send out direct mailing into specific target area (200, 500, etc.)

- Consultation

- Regular update of current market conditions

- Regular update of Comparative Market Analysis information

- Contact weekly by phone or e-mail

- Review all contract offers with recommendations

- Assist in negotiation of contract

- Be present at home inspection

- Be present for lender appraisal if possible

- Coordinate details of setting up settlement

- Be present at settlement

country and is the norm in most areas. This is particularly true in larger cities: the vast majority of prospective buyers will opt for buyer representation.

The obvious question, of course, is "Who pays for this?" In the past a purchaser who wished to have buyer representation would have been obligated to pay for this service at whatever rate was established by the broker. As buyer agency became more popular throughout the country, it was determined that payment itself was not the criterion for establishing which party was represented by the agent.

A brokerage relationship is established with a client by means of a signed contract. This is a common procedure on the listing side; few agents would start marketing a new listing without having a signed listing agreement from the seller. The same procedure should apply for a buyer client. In order to establish the brokerage relationship, the client should sign an Exclusive Right to Represent Buyer Broker/Agency agreement. In this agreement an amount is stated that will be due to the agent when a satisfactory property has been found and purchased. The agreement also states that any payment made to the agent through the transaction will be credited against the amount due. In other words, at the time of settlement, the seller pays the agreed-upon commission to his or her listing broker, the listing broker pays the amount offered through the MLS to a cooperating broker (buyer agent), and the selling broker pays the agent. Payment is made through the transaction, not directly out of the seller's pocket. Remember, until there is a bonafide purchaser, there is no money in the transaction.

What is the importance of buyer agency in niche marketing? It is everything! The very concept of "niche" market implies that these are *special* clients with *special* needs and they will need *special* attention—even more than any other group of potential purchasers. This would be difficult to achieve if the agent were working on the behalf of the seller. A problem sometimes arises when the niche market client has serious doubts about whether to sign the buyer agency agreement; there may be resistance or even suspicion on the part of the prospective client. This is especially true when working with someone from a different culture or with an older person who has not been involved in any real estate transaction for many years. In these cases, it may be helpful to provide a state or local association brochure that explains the concept of buyer agency. Printed material from a third-party source often adds credibility to what the agent is explaining.

IN REAL LIFE | Doris Barrell

One of my favorite expressions to use with potential clients is "Let me tell you how I work." I go on to say, "When I am working with a buyer, I feel it is absolutely necessary that I represent and act in the best interests of that buyer. I think you would agree that in a real estate transaction you would be much more comfortable knowing that I am always protecting and promoting your best interests and not that of the seller. The way we set up that relationship is with a written form called the Exclusive Right to Represent. Let me show you this form. It will explain exactly what my duties and responsibilities will be, and also how payment for my services will be made." After thoroughly reviewing the agency agreement, if the prospective client is still reluctant to sign, I suggest a short-term commitment—24 to 48 hours.

Difficult as it is to give up business, if prospects refuse to sign the buyer agency agreement under any circumstances, I decline to work with them.

The client must understand that the buyer agency agreement does bind the client to the agent. If the client does not honor the commitment and purchases a property through a different agent, the client may be liable for paying the commission themselves rather than the agent being paid through the transaction.

If a client seems to have reservations about making the buyer agency commitment, try one of these solutions:

1. Provide a clause in the agreement that it may be cancelled by the client with written notice at any time. (This would have to be approved by the broker.)

2. Suggest a time frame of only 24 or 48 hours. This way the agent clearly represents the buyer during the time they are looking at property. At the end of the 24 or 48 hours, the agreement may be extended or rewritten. Otherwise it becomes void.

Once your niche market is established and you are working primarily from a referral base, the problem of having the agreement signed should lessen. Past clients will be able to speak on your behalf about how the agreement has worked, how payment was actually made, and how you may be trusted to provide them with the good service that they deserve. Trust and confidence are the keys to establishing a well-established niche client referral base.

Other changes in the general brokerage business, such as discount brokers, salaried agents, and corporate brokerage ownership, may also have some impact on the niche marketer. The primary goal of niche marketing is to build a stable, loyal client base. This provides a degree of financial power to the individual real estate agent regardless of the financial arrangements or corporate management of the brokerage firm where niche marketers choose to place their license.

IN REAL LIFE | **Mark Nash**

Discount brokerage is a real competitor today with a full-service brokerage firm. In many markets the public has seen the value of properties and sale prices go up, while the percentage of compensation paid to their real estate agents and their firms stays fairly static overall. Adding to the public's concern is the relatively fast-moving seller's market in most areas of the country for the past several years. I think that consumers will start to look for ways to decrease their costs in the sale of their property. Discount brokerages are offering the consumer this option, and the number of listings represented by discounters is growing. This will obviously be an attraction to niche market members.

■ CONSUMER EXPECTATIONS

Today's consumers are far more knowledgeable than those in the past. It seems that everyone reads the weekly real estate section in the newspaper—and actually believes everything they read! In some ways this has made our agents' jobs easier, but in other cases newly self-appointed "experts" in real estate transactions can make life difficult for all concerned. And they often end up with a much worst deal than they could have had otherwise.

First-time homebuyers are generally young and have worked with computers in both their education and employment most of their lives. Thus, they often turn to the Internet to help them find and purchase their new home. Jim Barrell, husband of co-author Doris Barrell, tells a story about this (see "In Real Life").

IN REAL LIFE | Jim Barrell

First-time homebuyers Jack and Susan work with computers daily and insisted upon obtaining their mortgage loan through their own Internet research. They did not hesitate to sign a buyer representation agreement—in fact, they knew that they wanted an agent who would be representing their best interests at all times. Unfortunately, they did not carry that philosophy over to obtaining their mortgage loan. Despite my best efforts at encouraging them to at least talk to one of the local loan officers whom I have dealt with successfully, they were dead set on doing their financing through the Internet. Since they were very open about their plans, finances, and so on, it was not a case of protecting their privacy as much as being almost a game with them to do the research and work with an Internet lender. There are some fine on-line mortgage lenders, and I know of many cases where the borrower has received both good service and a good deal; however, this did not turn out to be one of those cases.

One of the numerous problems was that an appraisal was not ordered until three days before the proposed settlement, and it came in $10,000 low due to the appraiser using inappropriate and out-of-date comps. (The buyer and seller had to each pay $5,000.) Two days before settlement it was discovered that the mortgage company was not licensed to work in Virginia, so the loan had to be transferred to a local company. Upon being told that this might delay settlement (for the third time), my buyer actually threatened to climb through the phone line and strangle the loan officer if their company did not settle as scheduled.

Although they did settle as scheduled, the loan has a *six percent prepayment penalty,* over four years! The settlement attorney was so astounded that he offered to go after the company on his own time. He may very well win the case, because the borrowers were never given either a Good Faith Estimate or Truth-in-Lending Statement as required by RESPA.

Fortunately, both the buyers and sellers are very pleasant people and they were able to work out most of the minor glitches between themselves. The buyer was even gracious enough to tell me that they certainly should have listened to me in the first place!

■ THE INTERNET: FRIEND OR FOE?

When the Internet first became a viable source for locating information about purchasing a home, many felt that the days of the real estate agent were limited. The public is able to find a great deal of information about properties for sale through the Internet: over two million listings appear every day on www.realtor.com and numerous other company and individual Web sites. Real estate agents are no longer the sole source of information for prospective buyers; information is available everywhere. What the real estate professional offers today is service. This is not service in the sense of locating property, but service in guiding the buyer through the multilayered process of purchasing a home. Enter the niche marketer, whose entire focus is on providing extraordinary service.

■ MEETING EXPECTATIONS IN BOTH HOT AND COLD MARKETS

When the market is hot like in San Francisco, Boston, and Washington, D.C., in the early 2000s, there may be ten, fifteen, or even more contracts offered on one listing within days of the property being placed on the market. Making your client's offer the most attractive is a tricky process that may require the use of an escalation clause, the waiving of any type of contingency, or other creative ways. Introducing the prospective buyers to the seller can sometimes smooth the way for a successful transaction. For example, there was a recent case in Montgomery County, Maryland, where the sellers ratified a contract that was actually $20,000 below the highest offer because the sellers related very strongly to the purchasers. The prospective buyers had a handicapped child, and the house was well adapted for the child's use.

There is no substitute for an experienced real estate professional in this type of market. The sales agent that takes the time to really know and understand the wants and needs of the buyer clients will be in a much better position to negotiate with the listing agent and the sellers.

Looking at the hot market from the seller's side, it is obvious that average sellers would be totally at a loss to cope with fifteen offers coming in at the same time on their property. The simple logistics of how to have the offers presented becomes a real problem, much less how to handle counters, determine the prime contract, and provide for backup contracts. In many cases the sellers would simply accept the highest offer. Sellers need and should expect the objective consultation services of their agent to determine the best all-around offer, not merely the highest bid.

On the other hand, in a slow time when there are twenty times more listings available than there are buyers, someone needs to be able to prepare a negotiation strategy that will work to achieve the best results for a buyer. In this type of market, buyers may fall in love with a house and end up paying far more than necessary without a calm, objective agent to guide them. In a slow market, sellers need help in determining what exactly will make their home show better and be more attractive to potential buyers. Sometimes this takes a substantial amount of input of time and money. Rooms may need to be painted, clutter must always be removed, yards may require mowing or new plantings, and old appliances may need to be replaced. In a slow market, the property has to be both the prettiest and the best buy on the block to ensure a quick sale at a favorable price. Sellers need to rely on the expertise of their agent. In addition, working with a particular niche group may require other special considerations. Providing extraordinary service is not an easy task!

■ THE IMPACT OF CULTURE

Consumer expectations also vary according to the individual buyer or seller's own background. Depending on how business is conducted in their home country, the immigrant purchaser or seller may expect more of their agent than can be legally achieved. Sometimes purchasers think they can still negotiate for items to be conveyed with the property or provided as extras long after the contract has been ratified. Sellers who do not understand United States legalities may have ratified a contract but then decide they want to sell to someone else who said they would offer more. You may run into either buyers or sellers who want to continue negotiating the price right up to the settlement table. When agents try to explain that this is not the way business is done in the U.S., consumers may feel frustrated in their expectations.

■ THE LAW VS. EXPECTATIONS

Property disclosure is an area where conflict of law versus expectation sometimes occurs when working with a senior client. Most states today require some type of disclosure of material adverse defects in the property. This may not mean much to a 70-year-old seller who was never told about that basement leak when he bought the house forty years ago. He may see no reason to disclose that the basement still leaks and tell his agent, "You had better not mention it to any buyers now!"

Fair Housing Law is another area that may cause a problem in meeting consumer expectations. Sellers may want to restrict who will be allowed to buy their house. Buyers may want to ask questions about the racial or ethnic makeup of a neighborhood. When the agent tries to explain that both disclosure and fair housing are areas covered by federal and state law, it may appear to the clients that their agent is not living up to the promised expectation of totally representing the client's best interests. For more information and examples of fair housing questions, see Appendix A.

■ PART-TIME VS. FULL-TIME AGENTS

The National Association of REALTORS® recently reported that approximately one-third of active agents today are considered to be part-time. Different states have various interpretations of what constitutes a full-time practitioner. In Virginia, for example, a salesperson must have been actively engaged in real estate practice for forty hours per week for a period of three years before taking the broker license exam. This would seem to imply that a part-time agent would never be eligible for a broker license.

IN REAL LIFE | Doris Barrell

In my last office three of the top-producing agents were in the part-time category: two were teachers and one worked for the government. Their production was consistently above that of many of the so-called full-time agents in the office. All three were single and devoted all of their free time to their real estate business. I certainly would never have refused to have them in my office, nor did I ever consider them to be part-time agents.

An important element in their success was that they all worked a special niche. One is a police officer whose niche market is made up of her fellow police officers. Another is a high school math teacher who works with other teachers from her own school and the lower grade schools that feed into that high school. The third works for the Census Department of the U.S. government. Always able to provide helpful resource information, he concentrates his niche market on the other young singles and recently married first-time homebuyers whom he knows through his office connection.

The problem here is in defining *part-time*. Many companies will not accept any agent who has a full-time job elsewhere. However, many part-time agents are highly productive (see "In Real Life").

■ RELATIONSHIP SELLING KNOWS NO GEOGRAPHY

Some larger cities in the U.S. straddle two state lines. Agents in those cities are usually licensed in both jurisdictions. For example, many agents in the Washington Metro area are licensed in Maryland, District of Columbia, and Virginia. The necessity to be licensed in more than one jurisdiction may be particularly true when dealing with your own special niche market. Whether your niche is with immigrants, seniors, first-time homebuyers, gays or lesbians, the handicapped, a specific ethnic group, or any other specialized market, they do not all necessarily live in the same geographic area. Niche marketing relates to people, not places.

■ CONCLUSION

For many years it made sense for the local real estate brokerage firm to be a central figure in communities across our country. But as our population expanded, and we became more mobile as a society, relocation started the detachment of real estate from the local brokerage office and the local economy. When third-party relocation companies began to long-distance manage properties, agents, and transferees, it started a paradigm shift from local to global in residential real estate. Many international real estate companies have understood this and have profited from it.

Only recently, with the broad acceptance of the Internet, have real estate sales agents realized how global our business has become. When an agent receives an e-mail from someone out of the area requesting information on a listing seen on an Internet Web site, it shows how far-reaching our business has become. Potential clients today may be coming from anywhere in world. Relationship selling is the next large step for real estate sales professionals to embrace in order to be part of the consumer-driven transformation taking place in the real estate industry today.

2

Understanding Consumer Products Marketing

The practice of real estate is not the only business to have seen major changes in the past few years. In fact, the entire marketing industry has made quantum leaps in the effort to reach out to potential consumers and to develop a better understanding of the target audience. This Chapter will take a brief look at the history of consumer products marketing and the changes in marketing techniques in recent years. Understanding these changes in the overall marketing field should help you establish a basis on which to build marketing plans for your special niche market. At the end of the chapter you will find "Steps to Niche Marketing Success," a step-by-step program to help you select, develop, and profit from your own individual niche market. These steps are part of an overall business plan (as discussed in Chapter Five) but are listed separately to illustrate ways to implement the subject material of each particular chapter.

When we first met to develop the general outline for this book, it soon became apparent that niche marketers can learn from the concepts developed earlier for consumer products marketing. Our initial conversation went something like this:

> *Doris:* Mark, as you know, I have been involved in real estate marketing for over twenty years, but I don't have any background in other types of consumer products marketing. I'm sure your life-before-real-estate marketing background, where you represented companies like Clairol and Duracell, taught you a great deal on this subject. Can you tell me more about this?

> *Mark:* Consider "soap operas," that is, marketing by combining a consumer product with a recreational activity. An early niche market for detergent manufacturers was the viewer of daytime televised dramas. The manufacturer sponsored the soap operas, and the loyal audience consumed their products. The viewer demographics have evolved from the early days, and have spun off other subniches such as Hispanic and African-American daytime drama viewers. Many products other than soap are now being advertised through that medium.

> *Doris:* The reference to the soap operas certainly rings a bell for me. In my attempts to learn Spanish I was advised to watch the daytime "novellas" (Spanish "soaps"). I can see that advertisers would greatly benefit from promoting their products with this popular audience. But what about the deluge of ads on prime-time TV, or the twelve-section newspaper that you can hardly carry into the house on Sunday mornings?

Mark: The saturation of ads received by potential consumers is a real issue for marketers. The consumer either bonds with or dismisses a marketing message in a very short period of time. Niche marketers attempt to establish a relationship with the consumer to drive brand loyalty and consumption. Let's look at this small window of time to establish bonding and apply it to our real estate business. When I'm showing property to buyers, I can tell within the first few minutes whether we have begun to bond. The first time out on showings is a very quick study if I have read my clients correctly in their home search. Multiple home inventory tours with no resulting bonding will never establish a good agent/client relationship. Nothing will be able to overcome misreading the information and feedback the potential homebuyers can give you. In fact, they will most likely look for a new agent to represent them. Listening, assimilating, and bonding are the key ingredients for any consumer marketer.

Doris: That certainly makes sense. In fact, that is probably what most good real estate agents do without even realizing that they are not only trying to sell a house, but are actually developing a relationship with the client that leads to brand loyalty with the agent or company.

■ AFFIRMING THE INDIVIDUAL

Affirming of the individual consumer is an important element of specialized marketing. Advertising and other marketing programs that appear to understand the wants and needs of the particular consumer are much more likely to be well-received and acted upon. Consumers today want to feel special and will pay more attention to marketing that appears to be developed especially for them. This makes it essential to carefully test the results of any marketing program as it is presented through various media sources. As the best means of reaching out to the preselected group is determined, the niche market begins to develop. Once trust and confidence are established with the original core of niche consumers, there are additional benefits.

There is no better marketing than a satisfied customer. Every one of those individuals reached through the initial marketing program knows others in the same niche category. Word of mouth begins to build the reputation of both product and provider. A second benefit is that it may now become possible to consider cross-marketing of other products to the same niche. In the soaps world this could mean selling hair products, cosmetics, and so forth, in addition to detergent. In the real estate world this could include mortgage lending, homeowner warranties, settlement services, and relocation referrals.

■ CHANGES IN MARKETING IN THE LAST TEN YEARS

Consumers have been bombarded with advertising messages through traditional media channels such as television, radio, and print since the early 1950s. The 1990s added messages from the Internet, cable, fax, telemarketing, and direct mail. The number and frequency of advertising messages delivered to consumers have also increased to levels where consumers have become oversaturated. Marketers had to rethink how to reach consumers. One theory was to target specific or niche groups that shared a common interest. Marketers also discovered that members of target groups perceived products and their value to themselves differently from each other. So "one size fits all" in consumer products marketing evolved into target or niche marketing.

■ UNDERSTANDING TARGET AUDIENCES

With consumers being bombarded by messages, marketers realized they needed better ways to reach them. Instead of force-feeding their messages, marketers decided to learn more about the consumer. Marketers in the 1990s began to reinforce the association between their product and the potential consumer's lifestyle, ethnic background, hobbies, interests, and so on. They reinforced their familiarity with the consumer by focusing their messages to the target audience or niche. Print ads began to reflect their audiences: Hispanics received Spanish-language ads, African-Americans saw African-American models, gay and lesbian consumers observed same-gender visuals. The consumers reacted by consuming manufacturers' products that identified with them. No longer were the niche consumers ignored, they were celebrated! The niche consumer responded with brand loyalty, something that has been decreasing through the early 1990s.

■ BRAND LOYALTY

Brand loyalty has dropped in the last ten years as more product options have become available to the consumer. Although some consumers continue to buy the same products that they have known and loved for years, many others now turn to generic brands or chain-store products that cost less. Do you still always reach for Coca-Cola, Kleenex, Del Monte canned peas, or Windex? Or are you more likely to take whatever on the shelf that is cheaper? Many shoppers today will happily give up their manufacturer's coupons in order to shop at a warehouse club where lower overhead costs are passed on as savings to the consumer.

What can product marketers do today to improve their customer loyalty? The ebb and flow of consumer emotions dictates their buying habits. Marketers' answers to maintaining brand loyalty from the consumer has to start with listening to, assimilating, and updating information received from consumers in order to know what they are looking for. Whether consciously or not, consumers are constantly evaluating their personal perceptions and consumption patterns of products. Product marketers must now educate their consumers to the value of the product in order to keep customer loyalty.

■ KNOW THE CONSUMER

The major change in consumer product marketing in the 1990s was the move from the general sales pitch of "Buy our product" to the specific "Our product is like you, your lifestyle, or special interest." By building familiarity with the consumer, marketers make the decision to purchase easier for the consumer. The affirmation of consumers also builds brand loyalty. Consumers identify with products that identify with them. They are more sophisticated today and recognize marketing that tries to manipulate them versus affirming them. Target or niche consumers look for companies attempting to affirm them through corporate programs such as affirmative action, environmental safety, domestic partnership benefits, and other programs that internally support their external target or niche consumers. Consumers view these internal policies as proof that the company has a true vested interest in the niche consumers they're attempting to affirm.

■ SPECIALIZED VS. GENERAL MARKETING

General marketing uses the old concept of throwing spaghetti at the wall to see what sticks. Specialized marketing directed to target or niche markets focuses the marketer's pitch to a specific audience. Measuring response from input (advertising) to output (sales) makes it easier for marketers to continue or change messages to the niche. Many consumer product companies today have a multitude of niches they target with specific messages rather than general marketing aimed at everyone.

■ QUALIFYING YOUR CONSUMER NICHE

Marketers test many niches that could become part of their media plans. They also test the various media channels to best reach their target niches. The gay and lesbian niche was one of many in the 1990s that became the focus of some marketers. They pursued this niche because of its generally high disposable income and consumption of quality and luxury products. Because of changing societal attitudes toward this niche, marketers could now openly target it in special-interest media to promote their products. Liquor, automobile, computer, and other manufacturers courted gays and lesbians. Within the niche the response was mixed. Some felt they were finally affirmed as a consumer group with specific needs, but others felt they were being exploited by corporate America. Ultimately, the companies that felt it profitable to market to this niche supported the niche and the niche accepted the company as acting ethically towards the niche (see "In Real Life").

IN REAL LIFE | Mark Nash

In the mid 1990s national consumer product manufacturers started to segment their advertising in order to reach the gay and lesbian market. Their focus was print ads in gay and lesbian national magazines and local newspapers. At first the community responded to the ads favorably. The assumption was that these companies realized the attractive demographic of the gay and lesbian consumer. After the initial validation wore off, the community started to delve deeper into the manufacturers' overall position on gays and lesbians. Did the company offer partnership benefits to employees that were in same-gender relationships? Did the advertising visuals present same gender couples in place of their typical ad photos? Many in the community realized that the manufacturers were looking for increased sales without backing up their commitment with real internal or external policies concerning gays and lesbians. When the community could not substantiate sincere motivation on the part of the manufacturer, political members of the community initiated product boycotts. Some manufacturers realized that if a niche were to support their product, they would have to have corporate policies backing up their interest in the niche.

■ CROSS-MERCHANDISING

Once marketers have established a relationship with their consumers, they can begin to pitch other products to them, based on the niche trust. The other products related to their core brands are cross-merchandised based on the existing relationship between the consumer and the original product. It is much easier and less expensive for consumer product manufacturers to remarket to existing consumers than to develop new ones. As the consumer feels increasingly comfortable with one product, it becomes easier to extend that level of comfort to marketing additional products.

For example, real estate salespersons establish a relationship with the consumer in listing their property or locating a property for them to purchase. The broker can then cross-merchandise home warranties, mortgage loans, settlement services, insurance, and other services. Some of the larger real estate firms today are experimenting with cross-merchandising additional products, such as automobiles, furniture, and household appliances, to their real estate niche consumer. This is an example of how the real estate business has learned some valuable lessons from general consumer product marketing strategies.

Several Internet-based mortgage companies have already realized the value of the relationship that real estate sales agents have with their clients. Under RESPA guidelines in some states it is legal for agents to receive a fee from a mortgage company for originating a mortgage if they perform a required number of steps in the mortgage loan process. Internet mortgage companies realize that the agent has a first-line relationship with the consumer that can help them sell their mortgage product.

Home warranties have been a natural cross-sell for many years. Mortgage loans companies take the cross-sell to one more component of the transaction by offering to provide other financial services to the customer. The banking industry recognizes this opportunity, as evidenced in current lobbying attempts to allow banks to offer real estate brokerage services to their mortgage customers. As they have already established relationships with account holders at their financial institution, they would like to cross-sell real estate brokerage in addition to other financial services that they offer.

■ PRESELLING

Once you have established a base and reputation within a niche, that niche starts to presell you or your product. Word of mouth promotes your affirmation of them and sells you to future clients. The presell is cost effective and saves valuable time in acquiring new clients. Your phone ringing with new clients that your current or past clients have presold is definitely an efficient way to build your real estate sales business. Give your clients the tools to presell you and you will be rewarded with a growing base of new loyal clients. You will find that it is possible to built trust with them in a much shorter period of time.

■ TESTING

Because of the cost of advertising today, marketers do thorough testing to get the response rate they need for profitability. Testing a variety of messages in both text and graphics to see which has a higher consumer response rate allows the marketer to see which message receives the highest level of sales. Testing is a tried and true method of consumer response and is based on statistical models. Direct response testing looks for a response from the consumer in just one ad. Manufacturers drop coupons in the Sunday paper to initiate trial usage of their products to secure future brand and product consumer loyalty.

IN REAL LIFE | Mark Nash

The Internet has made a significant impact on real estate: brokerage firms, the Multiple Listing Service, and REALTOR® associations all have a major Internet presence. Agent Web sites, also growing in popularity, focus on an agent's community, professional background, and listing information. In the Internet world I have taken a more relationship-based view of my niche-based Web site, www.outrealty.com. I do not promote listings. However, I do offer gay and lesbian relocation service and real estate resources to establish and provide site visitors with added value in place of a direct pitch to sell property. Testimonials from previous gay and lesbian clients presell site visitors on my real estate sales services. I cross-merchandise outrealty.com on my general Web site, www.marknashrealtor.com to increase awareness of my niche site. The best part of having a 24/7 presence on the World Wide Web is the e-mail requests for information from people all over the United States—and even the world—to help them in their move, develop relationships with them, and receive referrals from them. It works for me in my niche market; it can certainly work for you in yours.

Marketers also test visual graphics of the people, ad colors, et cetera, in their print or television ads to gauge what motivates the consumer to try or repurchase their product. If direct-mail advertising has not worked, try experimenting with different formats to increase the level of response.

■ INTERNET ADVERTISING

The Internet has obviously changed many things in our daily life today, both at home and in business. For students and instructors, the Internet is a tremendous resource. For many people today e-mail has virtually replaced "snail mail." However, this valuable addition to our lives does not come without certain aggravations. Having to wade through 50 or 60 e-mail messages every day in order to get to the four or five that are of interest to you is both time-consuming and annoying.

Direct marketers using any media, whether e-mail, snail mail, telemarketing, or other means, purchase lists from companies who mission is to compile and update the lists and keep them viable. Once you have an e-mail address, it becomes part of a list file. Supposedly, you now avoid the phone ringing during dinner with a sales pitch but instead receive the sales pitch at your convenience through your e-mail. Although there are many pros and cons involved, the Direct Marketing Association strongly lobbies for the right to allow all reasonable forms of marketing.

■ CONCLUSION

An understanding of the changes occurring in general consumer products marketing over the past decade helps establish a foundation on which to build our ideas for the marketing of real estate. Real estate marketing may be for a product (house, retail store, condominium, rental project), for a brokerage firm, or for an individual agent. A variety of techniques may be used for the marketing of a property, a company, or a sales practitioner, but an important aspect to the marketing should be the affirmation of the prospective customer. This is achieved though a shift from emphasizing the "what" is being marketed to the "who" is to be the recipient of the message. An aggressive testing program makes it possible to determine if the marketing is in fact reaching those to whom it is directed. Once you have determined your target audience, you are ready to begin planning a direct marketing program that will best reach out to those special individuals.

■ STEPS TO NICHE MARKETING SUCCESS

Consumer Product Advertising Self-Study

1. Choose a national niche consumer marketing campaign that advertises heavily in your market area. Identify the niche by demographic; for example, age, gender, ethnicity, religion, lifestyle, income, and geography (urban, suburban, rural).

2. Find examples of niche-specific advertising from each of the following media: magazines, newspapers, direct mail, radio, television, cable, Internet/Web sites.

3. Analyze from each media how the advertising targets the specific niche audience:

    A. Written copy (print and Internet only): generic, niche specific?

    B. Ad visuals: (1) Use of color, lack of color; list two strongest colors. (2) Use of niche relative photos/graphics? (3) Type/font style, size; is ad heavy with or light on type?

    C. Is it consumer interactive? Does it make consumers proactive versus reactive? Make them feel good about product? Does it turn off consumers with non-niche photos or graphics? Does it accurately portray niche?

1. Does it engage niche consumer to act? Find out additional information? Decide to purchase? Decide not to purchase? Decide to boycott product?

2. Does it promote word of mouth within niche? Make niche consumer tell a friend? Make niche consumer *not* want to tell a friend? Make niche consumer complain to fellow niche consumer about misrepresenting niche?

D. Consumer-niche take-away: Does it provoke a response, or present product? Positive, neutral, or negative response? Informational or specific product pitch? Do messages change from one media form to another? Do niche consumer reactions change from one medium to another? Is there an obvious theme in the campaign? Is the message clear?

1. If you were a niche member, how would you react to these ads?

   a. Purchase

   b. Gather more information before making decision

   c. Not purchase

2. What is your own take-away from this focused niche marketing advertising?

3

Niche versus Traditional Farming

"Old McDonald had a farm, e-i-e-i-o ...." What exactly do we mean by the term *farming* in the real estate business? Actually it is not that different from actual farming: first you plant the seeds, then water and fertilize, weed as needed, and hopefully those seeds will someday result in a bountiful harvest. In the real estate world those seeds are initial contacts, watering and fertilizing is provided through the use of various means of contact, weeding is keeping accurate up-to-date files on the farm area, and the harvest consists of prospective clients and customers. The traditional real estate farm usually consisted of 300 to 500 names of people in a certain geographic area. It could, of course, also be a list of names taken from the agent's own sphere of influence. A sphere of influence is made up of people the agent knows directly or indirectly through membership in a club, church, sports group, or other organization. To anyone who has been in the real estate business for more than 10 years, the following should sound very familiar.

■ MS. MCDONALD BUYS THE FARM

Sally Eager Beaver has just obtained her real estate license and signed on with Bob Broker. Full of spirit and enthusiasm, she eagerly shows up at 9:00 A.M. on her first day to meet with him. His initial training program (after pointing out her desk and phone) sounds something like this:

"Okay, Sally, pick yourself out a neighborhood. Then get out there and collect all the information you can about the shopping, transportation, civic groups, places of worship, schools, playgrounds, and anything else particular to that neighborhood. Pull up the tax records and put together a book with all the city or county information available on each house in the neighborhood. Then get yourself some good walking shoes and start knocking on doors. Get out there to meet and greet everyone in the farm you pick.

It wouldn't be a bad idea to take along a little something to leave with them, like a ball-point pen, refrigerator magnet, or maybe a calendar of events for that neighborhood. Good luck, and call me when you get a listing!"

Did this type of geographic farming work? In many cases it did. Faithful seeding and nurturing brought a steady stream of business for many dedicated agents over a period of years. However, many of those seeds were spread with no guarantee of who was going to reap the harvest. Ask yourself honestly: Before you were in the real estate business yourself, how many of those flyers, newsletters, recipe cards, and even calendars that you received went straight into the wastebasket? Studies indicate that the return on direct mail advertising is somewhere below two percent. Wouldn't it make more sense to direct all of that time,

IN REAL LIFE | Doris Barrell

My office was located in the Mount Vernon area of Alexandria, Virginia. This is essentially a suburb of Washington, D.C., and is made up of many neighborhood subdivisions. We had a huge map posted on the wall that had all of these communities clearly marked. As each community was selected for farming by one of my agents, I stuck a push-pin in the middle of that area with the agent's name attached. Agents could also pick one of the many condominium projects found in that area. New agents who joined the office were invited to select one of the areas that was not currently covered. As a matter of courtesy (not law—that might violate antitrust, fair housing, or other laws), new agents refrained from farming a subdivision that was already covered. As I conducted my annual review sessions with each agent, we discussed what progress the agent was making with his or her farm. If an agent was neglecting the farm—no mailings, no visits, no phone calls, no business—someone else was encouraged to take over that particular farm area.

energy, and money formerly spent on developing a geographic area into building relationships with potential clients?

Remember the philosophy of directed consumer products advertising: Direct your marketing to those whom you already know may be interested in your product.

■ THE NEW CONSUMER

Consumers are increasingly sophisticated in the process of selling and buying real estate. Average sale prices in most markets are high enough that a free pen or refrigerator magnet will not motivate a $300,000 buyer to cold call or e-mail a real estate agent. Today's consumer perceives real estate as an investment or savings/retirement vehicle. How many financial planners, CPAs, or tax attorneys send their clients recipe cards? These professionals typically send clients monthly newsletters containing valuable information concerning the current financial market. Most of these newsletters do not have a direct sales pitch, but suggest that you call for more information or if you have questions. This type of marketing is directed at establishing long-term relationships rather than a quick sale or purchase of investment products.

This is not to say that traditional farming cannot work. However, all of that effort will produce better results when you direct it at a particular niche market. Sending out a 3,000-piece mailer looking for buyers may produce one or two new clients. What if those 3,000 pieces were directed to a targeted group of people based on common interests, rather than to a list of addresses? Most likely, at the end of the day you would have more new potential clients for the same expenditure of time and money.

Stepping back, we need to study the message being presented in order to determine why the mailer does or does not make any impact. Many mail-out pieces make a direct pitch for the agent, as in "I sold a property in the neighborhood" or "I just listed a property." If the consumer already has a relationship with another agent, why would a "just listed" or "just sold" card motivate the consumer to call this new agent? An added value to the mailing, such as a study of neighborhood appreciation over the past few years (in addition to the just-listed/sold tag line), might signal to the recipient that the agent is business and market knowledgeable and takes a big-picture approach to marketing. Adding value, without an overt sales pitch, communicates that the REALTOR® is more interested in establishing a long-term relationship with the consumer than in a quick sale.

IN REAL LIFE | Mark Nash

"What do you mean, you're not going to have a farm?" asked the highest-producing agent in my first real estate office. My response was that I would have a relationship list that covered many communities in the larger market versus the town my real estate sales office was in. "Good luck," the agent responded. So I set out to work my relationship list. contacts at businesses, organizations, and social groups that were owned by gays or lesbians or friendly to them. I discussed with people on my list the needs and demographics of the suburban Chicago gay and lesbian community. At some point in the conversation I was usually asked what I did for a living. I told them that I was a sales associate with a local brokerage firm. This was a low-key, non-overt sales pitch. Many people remembered what I did and where I practiced and began to refer their real estate business to me. Each month my list, business, and conversations grew. Eighteen months later I was named individual sales leader of the year in my 40-agent office. The former highest-producing agent congratulated me on my sales success. She added, "I don't know much about this gay and lesbian stuff, but I'm thinking about changing my marketing perspective to drive my business!"

THE UNDER-30 CROWD

In the May, 2002 issue of REALTOR® magazine, published by the National Association of REALTORS®, there is an article about

30 bright agents under the age of 30. They are building great careers and became highly successful in just a few years. Many of them have done it through the traditional ways of cold calling, regular mailings, and knocking on doors. Some have concentrated their efforts on a higher level of technology, using Internet Web sites and e-mail to promote themselves and their listings. Over half of them, however, have developed specific niche markets, which seem to fall into three categories: a specific type of property, a particular group of people, or innovative financing programs.

Regarding the types of properties category, in some cases the new entrepreneurs had actually branched outside the residential field into industrial real estate or investment properties. This of course would require knowledge beyond the typical training of a residential agent. For example, one young man came from a family that had always invested heavily in single-family rental properties. It was only natural that he would find his niche in working with potential purchasers of such investment properties, offering them not only service in the searching for and purchasing of the property, but also in managing the property for them after the sale.

Several of the under-30 group are concentrating on new home developments, either as both construction and sale, or just sales. One has made his niche selling and renting luxury high-rise condos at the beach. One long-range planner started by concentrating on a fairly large condominium project. Then, as the new condo buyers needed more space, he began to develop a secondary niche in two nearby townhouse communities. We can guess what will come next: selecting several single-family detached-home communities for those move-ups from the townhouses.

■ FORECLOSURES

A foreclosed property is usually sad news for the people involved, but it has opened up a special niche opportunity. An agent knowledgeable about the problems involved in handing a foreclosure can develop a strong base of business in both the selling and the future purchase of the property. The key is developing strong relationships with attorneys, the lenders, and investment groups interested in purchasing such properties. Many homes are foreclosed by HUD and VA. Once an agent has learned how to wade through the typical government red-tape, this can become a terrific niche. Everyone is looking for a bargain these days.

A number of these young successful agents have concentrated their efforts on first-time buyers either through direct contact to apartment dwellers or by advertising special loan programs available for first-timers. Homebuyer seminars have always been popular as an office event, but agents are now conducting them on their own. One young woman specializes in brides. She puts on several bridal shows each year where she distributes invitations for her homebuyer seminars. Another young woman presents seminars in Spanish, and one enterprising young man gives seminars at Lowe's and Home Depot. Since reports tell us that the average new homeowner spends at least $2,000 in the first year, home improvement and fix-up stores should welcome such an innovative idea; perhaps they would even provide discounts or door prizes.

There are so many new financing programs today in addition to the traditional FHA loan for first-time homebuyers, that niche markets are being built around expertise in the down-payment assistance programs such as Nehemiah and Ameridream, FHA(203k) purchase and rehab loans, and zero-money-down programs. One of the entrepreneurs stated that he received more response from advertising a special *program* for the loan than for advertising a certain *house* for sale.

IN REAL LIFE | Doris Barrell

Reading about these wunderkind reminds me of an agent whom I trained last year. She lived in a condo and decided to make that her niche, specifically concentrating on the absentee owners. Washington, D.C., had gone through a number of years of a down market, especially for condos. Most of the absentee owners had no idea how much property values had increased and how much greater the demand was for property in the District. Cindy started a regular program of contacting these absentee owners and providing them current market information. Within weeks she had numerous listings in her building, which she very quickly sold. Of course, she made sure that the rest of the absentee owners plus those owners presently living in the condo got the good news about her success. This inevitably led to even more listings and sales. She has now expanded her efforts to two close-by condominiums, and I'm sure she will be equally successful there.

This entire "Under 30" article gives us great examples of agents finding underserved niches in the market and building a successful business from them. These young agents understand that you can't keep throwing spaghetti at the wall and hope something sticks. When we think about traditional farming versus niche marketing, we can look at it as reactive versus proactive marketing. The farmer sows his seeds and waits for the harvest (reactive approach). However, we all have bills to pay. How many of us can wait around for the possibility that the phone will ring? We need to *make* it ring, and ring with quality clients (proactive approach).

■ WE'RE IN THE PEOPLE BUSINESS

Some new agents say that they went into the real estate business because they "loved houses," "appreciated architecture," or "just wanted to help people." Artistic or altruistic reasons aside, residential real estate is obviously a vehicle in which personalities interact. Difficult negotiations are often more about the conflicting personalities of the sellers and buyers than about the actual property. How many times have we advised clients to keep their eye on the prize—the house—rather than winning a mind game with the seller? Will they ever interact again with these

IN REAL LIFE | Mark Nash

When I'm done silently screaming after I hear new agents talk about their appreciation for architecture, I could scream again when they tell me, "It's so much *fun* to go on tour and get out of the house!" I didn't get into the real estate sales business to get out of the house. What motivated me, as a sole supporter, was to run a business and make a living. This gives me a different perspective than some other agents. Increasingly I see in my market a professional business orientation in agents. Hooray! Let's look at the heading of this section: "We're in the People Business." It has two important words that every agent should understand about real estate sales—*people* and *business*. The architecture and getting out of the house are only the frosting on the agent's cake!

people? Probably not. And what percentage of the contract price is represented by that refrigerator that they are arguing over? Where in this picture is the love of houses or appreciation of architecture? Nowhere. Good agents must have the ability to relate to the clients, clarify the issues, and reason with difficult people to be successful in residential real estate sales.

■ FOCUS ON THE CONSUMER, NOT THE GEOGRAPHY

Keeping the two words *people* and *business* foremost in our minds, we can begin to leave the geography of real estate sales marketing and shift to consumer marketing. It is only natural to want to purchase any consumer product, whether it is an automobile or our first home, from someone we respect and who respects us. Consumers are more flexible, loyal, and communicative with salespeople when they both trust and respect them. Since respect is a relationship-based emotion, our goal must be to first create strong relationships with our clients. This is reversing the traditional mind-set of real estate professionals. We now want to look at potential clients based on relationships rather than geography.

Using our farming analogy, it seems that today instead of planting the seeds and waiting for them to grow, we can just step forward and selectively pick flowers from all the fields that already exist!

■ USING THE WEB

Most real estate companies today have their own Web sites, and many individual agents have taken the time and effort to set up Web sites of their own. The use of home computers continues to increase by leaps and bounds. More and more people

IN REAL LIFE | Mark Nash

"Trolling for clients" is what I call my using real estate sales Web site. Do I know where my next clients are? Are they in Paris, having just received the green light to relocate to my market? Do they have special needs that they saw referred to on my Web site? When they e-mail me to begin a possible business relationship, do I add value to their relocation? I couldn't have reached this potential client through traditional farming.

turn first to this convenient means of gaining information on almost every aspect of their day-to-day lives. Having your own Web site gives you an opportunity to present your special interests and abilities that make you a perfect match for members of your target niche.

■ CONCLUSION

The essential aspect of niche marketing is to develop and build on relationships with people, not geography. The quantum leaps in technology today have made it possible to maintain a database that can be accessed and updated in minutes. Every potential client can be reached in minutes through e-mail. Attractive Web sites can attract thousands of prospects with a click of a button. We can do it faster, we can do it better. The point is to do it effectively and to develop a message that has meaning to the particular group that you are attempting to reach. Save the seeds for the prepared patch of ground instead of sowing them all over the vast field.

STEPS TO NICHE MARKETING SUCCESS

Geographic Farm Approach

1. List or define your geographic farm in your market area by number of households.

2. Determine how many other agents in your office have the same farm households. Determine how many other agents in your market from outside your office have the same farm households.

3. Calculate the number of direct mail or telemarketing hits each household in your farm receives from all agents in your market each month, each quarter, and each year.

4. Save and review samples of direct-mail pieces from all agents in your farm geography.

5. Which direct-mail pieces do you think work best? Why?

6. Which pieces add the most value to the consumer? Which pieces make the consumer want to respond? What is your ratio of direct-mail pieces sent to closed transactions yearly?

7. Calculate the time per mailing you spend, include copy-writing, printing, addressing, applying postage, and mailing. Calculate the expense of each mailing, including each of those steps.

Niche Marketing Approach

1. List and define two specific niches you could market to.

2. How many agents market to the same niches?

3. How many agents outside of your office market to the same niches? Review samples of marketing pieces from other agents marketing to these niches.

4. Decide how you could add value to each niche and otherwise differentiate yourself from others marketing to those niches.

5. Calculate the time you need to invest in each niche, for example, attending meetings, networking events, building relationships, and doing referral-related communication. Calculate the amount of expense reaching these niches, including advertising, transportation expenses, and so forth. Project the ratio of your first-year closed transactions versus expense and time to market to each niche.

6. Project your personal and professional sense of satisfaction from giving back to niche.

4

Identifying Your Niche

In the previous Chapter we talked about the advantages of niche marketing versus the traditional geographic, or sphere-of-influence, farming. Many people entering the real estate business today, especially the ones sometimes referred to as the "young turks" (because of their aggressive new ways of handling their business), see the traditional methods of farming as being old-fashioned and out-of-date in today's computer-based society. If you are interested in exploring the possibilities of achieving more financial power through niche marketing, the first step is to determine your own special niche.

First, let's take a look at some of the possible categories for a niche market, beginning with some that we are most familiar with. Depending on your local market or your own personal interest, you can probably think of other possibilities.

■ SENIOR CITIZENS

Demographic studies show that by the year 2020, one-third of the population of the United States will be over the age of 55. They are becoming an important force in the real estate market. Whether or not you decide to claim this as your niche, you will need to have a better understanding of working with this special group of clients and customers. There is a special designation for people who are concentrating their marketing efforts on senior citizens: the senior real estate specialist (SRES). More information, including the requirements to qualify for this designation and the locations of classes, may be found on www.sres.com.

The baby boomers (born between 1946 and 1964) caused a huge bulge in population demographics—sometimes described as looking like a snake that ate an elephant! This bulge of baby boomers has created a significant economic impact from the time they were born until the present. At first it was the creation of diaper service and easy-fix baby formula. Next, children attended classes in temporary trailers next to the schoolhouse. Then, those same kids graduated from their over-crowded high schools and found it difficult to get into college. Even worse, for probably the first time in history, we had college graduates who were not able to find a job.

Some people might say, "there are just too many boomers!" To those of us in the consumer marketing world, however, there is no such thing as "too many" consumers. The boomers are now in their most productive years, and the buying and selling habits of this group continues to have a strong impact on the real estate business. They may be looking for a second home near skiing, boating, or golf rather than a four-bedroom colonial in the suburbs, but this group of seniors is healthier, wealthier, and more mobile than any other group. They represent a great opportunity for the niche specialist.

IN REAL LIFE | Doris Barrell

Several years ago I was asking to prepare a class on "Serving the Senior Client." The class was to be used as part of continuing education credit for licensee renewal. In researching for this course, I learned that seniors actually fall into three distinct groups. The first, our oldest folks, are sometimes referred to as the "GI Generation"; they were born before 1925 and have lived through at least one world war, if not two. The next group (born between 1925 and 1945) is a relatively small group, but prospered through the post-World War II years and brought about significant social changes in the 1960s. The youngest of the seniors group, the "*rising* seniors," are the baby boomers (born between 1946 and 1964).

If you decide on seniors as your niche, your first step is to gain an understanding of the different needs and wants of each of the three sub-groups. For example, marketing to the oldest group of seniors might best be done through personal phone calls or visits. Direct face-to-face contact is very important with this group. As you move to the middle group, and especially to the "rising seniors" (baby boomers), more sophisticated forms of communication will probably be better received.

The middle group may enjoy monthly newsletters containing information about recent sales or properties for sale in their neighborhood. Many of the old farming techniques, such as sending out recipe cards, holiday greetings, sports schedules, or flags for Fourth of July, will still work very well with this group.

For the youngest group, boomers just starting to think about retirement, contact through Web sites and e-mail newsletters may be most effective. Information sent out only when there is something important or relevant, such as tax law changes or changing market conditions, will be much more impressive than a monthly mailing consisting of recipes and "Ask Heloise" types of tips.

■ IMMIGRANTS

Demographic studies also indicate that by 2025 one-third of our population will be people who have immigrated to our shores. Each culture, each ethnic group, and each nationality comes with its own special needs. No single agent can be expected to learn the customs and business practices of every group. Selecting one and developing a true rapport with that particular group is an effective way to build a basis for business that will increase through families and friends in a relatively short period of time.

U. S. Department of Commerce statistics show a volume of over 10 million people expected to immigrate to the United States in the first years of the 2000 decade. The greatest impact is in the gateway cities like Los Angeles, New York, San Francisco, Miami, Chicago, and Washington. Even small towns in the Midwest are seeing large waves of immigrant population growth. It is natural for people coming to this country to gravitate to a place where there are others who speak their language, understand their customs and habits, and are willing to assist the newcomers in finding jobs, education, and homes in their new land.

An agent who already speaks a second language is at a great advantage, but there is still a good opportunity for someone who is willing to take the time and energy needed to develop one of these immigrant groups as a niche market.

Largely due to the immigration factor, some major shifts are occurring in the traditional four categories of population demographics as gauged by the U.S. Census Bureau. The percentage of

IN REAL LIFE | Mark Nash

Did you know that there are more native Polish living in Chicago than in any other city in the world except Warsaw? Several enterprising agents have developed strong niche markets in this community. Consider Chinatown in San Francisco—actually a designated section of the city, identified on all city maps. Many older residents of Chinatown still speak no English. New York is sometimes referred to as the "capital of the world": almost every major ethnic group in the world (and dozens of smaller ones) has solid community roots there.

African Americans in 1990 was 12.5%; the projection for 2025 is 14.2%. A much larger increase is seen in the Hispanic group, which counted as 9% of the population in 1990 and is projected to be 16.8% by 2025—almost double. The largest percentage increase is in the Asian/Pacific Island category, which is projected to show a 150% increase, from 3% in 1990 to 7.5% by 2025.

Using the Internet and other advanced technology, even the novice niche marketer is now able to make contacts with people all over the world. Fannie Mae and Freddie Mac, the primary players in the mortgage loan secondary market, are pledged to provide more loan programs and funding for those in the "underserved" market, of which immigrants are a large part. Local lenders are learning how to deal with "mattress money" and private savings clubs in financially qualifying immigrant applicants. The smart niche marketer attends classes, interviews lenders, and stays current through Fannie Mae, Freddie Mac, and FHA Web sites to find out how best to help these new clients achieve their American dream of homeownership.

■ NATIONALITY

Learning about the special needs and interests of people from other countries is not limited to those recently coming to the U.S. Consider also first-generation or second-generation Americans who still maintain a high level of interest in and continuity of their own special cultures. Often, the first-generation or second-generation American prides himself or herself on doing business the "American way," but you may be surprised when it comes to important issues like marriage, funerals, and purchasing a home. Many of the old traditional customs and values seem to surface!

Feng shui has become an important buzzword today, not only in the Far Eastern community but also with Westerners. This fascinating study of how energy is gained, lessened, or even lost within a house has been important to Asian cultures for thousands of years. As we find ourselves serving more and more clients from these various national groups who believe wholeheartedly in following proper feng shui, the dedicated buyer agent must gain an understanding of how important this is to the client.

For the niche marketer this is not just something to enjoy reading about; this is an essential part of the service owed to the Asian client.

Just as we found that you cannot lump all seniors into one niche category, you will also find that you are making a grave error if you attempt to develop a niche market for "the Hispanics." You must determine whether you are talking about specializing in people from El Salvador, Peru, Argentina, Spain, Mexico, Cuba, or somewhere else that Spanish is spoken. Approximately one-fifth of the world population speaks some form of Spanish; you cannot specialize in all of them. If you do not already speak Spanish but intend to specialize in one par-

---

IN REAL LIFE | Doris Barrell

In my work with the International Real Property Foundation, I have the opportunity to travel to many countries that are attempting to build a real estate industry similar to ours. On a recent visit to Kuala Lumpur, Malaysia, and Bangkok, Thailand, I was shown several examples of good feng shui and how disastrous ignoring these beliefs can be. We visited one truly elegant office building—comparable to the best in contemporary architecture of New York, Chicago, or San Francisco. Almost the entire building sat empty—not because of economic downfall but because it was located next to a bridge over running water. Bad news for prospective tenants—fatal news for the developer.

---

ticular group, be sure to take Spanish lessons from someone familiar with that particular group's dialect and pronunciations.

■ GENDER

The Equal Credit Opportunity Act established that a married woman had the right to establish credit in her own name. A married woman can even purchase a property in her own name. The Virginia Slims motto "You've come a long way, baby" may be true, but it is still often difficult for a single woman, especially one who is the head of a household, to successfully purchase a home. Agents will soon attract a faithful following if they take time to seek out special programs and learn about antidiscriminatory lending practices.

■ SINGLE WOMEN HEADS OF HOUSEHOLDS

One of the most innovative ideas to come out of HUD in a long time is the recent "Section 8 to Homeownership." Under this program, any jurisdiction that presently receives HUD funding for the traditional Section 8 rental assistance program may now choose to convert some of those funds into assisting people to purchase a home rather than continue to rent. Each group makes its own determination as to how the funds are to be utilized, following HUD guidelines, of course. Nashville was one of the cities selected to take part in the pilot program for Section 8 to Homeownership. The housing assistance organization there decided to concentrate on single women who are heads of households. In one year they were able to place 13 families into home ownership, serving a very distinctive niche market!

■ COMMUNITY INTEREST ORGANIZATIONS

Community interest organizations cross many ethnic, national, and cultural lines. If you have a strong interest in community development, you might find your niche to be that of a local business executive's group or Chamber of Commerce. Some agents may consider their Rotary, VFW, or Kiwanis clubs to be their niche. Because the membership of these groups is more than likely extremely varied, the niche would not be so much centered on the persons themselves, as it would be on their special interest in serving the community.

■ PROTECTED CLASSES

The federal Fair Housing Law prohibits the denial of housing or services to anyone according to race, color, religion,

IN REAL LIFE | Larry Romito

I was working with a real estate firm in Florida where I discovered through research that there was a very large percentage of single female heads of households in that particular market area. After meeting with several focus groups, I determined that one of the major problems for these single moms was that they had no time to look for a new home because they held down full-time jobs. Another problem was what to do with the kids when the moms were out looking for a new home. They also shared a concern common to most first-time homebuyers: how to finance a home purchase. To respond to these concerns, my firm set up special home-buying and home-selling seminars especially designed for the working mom and led by other professional women and working mothers. The seminars were presented on Saturday mornings and even provided free baby-sitting services.

national origin, sex, familial status, or mental or physical handicap (see Appendix A). We have already mentioned senior citizens, immigrants, and people of different national origins. Another significant area for a special niche is serving those with disabilities. Agents throughout the country are now specializing in working with the hearing impaired. They are providing special phone systems and using e-mail for communication, learning sign language, and seeking out lenders and settlement agents who are also well-versed in working with this particular disability.

In some cases, real estate agents may have already been involved in working with a special group due to their own circumstances. Gradually these agents find that others from the

---

Marcia has been very active with a local group that works with children who suffer from Down's syndrome. She first became active in the group when her youngest child was born with this disability. Depending on the severity of the problem, many children with Down's, as they mature, are able to receive an education, hold down a job, and move into independent living. As Marcia's child grew older and was ready for this important step into independent living, Marcia found herself serving a new niche real estate market. Other parents from the group began to look to Marcia as the expert in locating housing suitable for the special needs of those with Down's syndrome. As she put it, she developed a niche through the back door.

---

group are turning to them for housing needs. These clients believe that their special problems will be understood and taken care of by agents who can truly empathize.

■ POLITICAL GROUPS

In Washington, D.C., there is a designated protected class of "Political Affiliation" under the D.C. Fair Housing Law. No landlord can refuse to rent to someone on the basis of political party. Generally, agents try to maintain a fairly neutral political posture, realizing that members of all parties do buy and sell houses. Conceivably, however, there could be a situation where there is an exceptionally hot political issue that the agent feels very strongly about, and the agent is willing to stand up for that position. In such a case the agent may appear to be establishing a niche made up of others who agree with the agent's position on the issue. Examples could be the no-growth issues that appear in rapidly expanding counties and cities, or environmental issues for protecting wilderness areas like forests in the Northwest or the Everglades. Such agents become known for a sincere belief in upholding the value system of the group even as they pursue their individual real estate practice. Of course, an agent should not ask questions about a prospective client's stand on political or environmental issues at an initial interview. This is a niche that is more likely to evolve as people become aware of the agent's personal feelings on the subject.

■ PROFESSIONAL NICHES

This niche often happens accidentally. For example, an agent may have a successful transaction with a doctor, lawyer, CPA, or other professional. The client appreciates the extra steps the agent has taken to work around busy schedules, to forgive cancelled appointments, and to step in whenever necessary to protect the client's interest when the client could not be there for an inspection or planned meeting. That satisfied client then mentions to colleagues that the perfect agent has been found! Other special niches today are those of working with police officers, firefighters, or teachers. Special programs like the FHA "Officer Next Door" are available throughout the country. Talk to your city, county, or state officials for specific information that will help you specialize in one of these groups of special people.

IN REAL LIFE | Doris Barrell

One of my new agents was a young woman married to a fire-fighter. Tonya was used to 48 hours on/3 days off, and other crazy schedules kept by those who protect our homes. Tonya could relate very well to the families of other firefighters. That quickly became her niche market. Her reputation spread from her husband's firehouse to many others within the county and she was soon well on her way to a successful real estate career.

Another new agent was a police officer in Alexandria. He was concerned at first over whether I would mind if he occasionally drove his police cruiser to the office. On the contrary, I never felt safer! He, too, had a crazy schedule. However, he was able to develop a niche market within the police community, showing properties to his fellow officers when they had their days off, working around abrupt changes in schedule due to emergencies, and understanding their particular concerns about neighborhood reception.

■ SPIRITUAL

Sometimes an agent will say, "I don't feel comfortable seeking business from members of my church or congregation." Well, why not? Most people would prefer to work with someone they already know and trust. Obviously, no one wants to be seen as pushy or inappropriately soliciting business in the place of worship. Whether or not you are actually a member of a particular church, synagogue, or mosque, there are ways to show your respect to the members. Something as simple of being aware of usual times and days of worship or knowing the dates and cus-

IN REAL LIFE | Mark Nash

After deciding to market to a niche, I considered underserved or invisible consumer groups in the suburban Chicago area. After completing some research, I discovered that the suburban gay and lesbian community was not being marketed to for their real estate needs. The community was spread over six counties, some with protective class laws and some without protections. On the whole I did not hear of much discrimination, but I did hear of a lack of sensitivity to the specific needs of the community. Many gays and lesbians wanted to be "out" with their real estate sales agents; they didn't want to introduce their partner as their "decorator" or "friend." These gays and lesbians wanted to be recognized as individuals or couples, with the same housing needs and desires as other buyers and sellers. Gay and lesbian real estate consumers appreciated the affirmation and understanding I brought to their transactions.

toms of special religious holidays helps create an impression that you are a real estate professional who both understands and respects the client's religion.

This could be particularly significant in working with a group that is not as well-known as American Baptist or Roman Catholic. Learning, understanding, and respecting the special concerns of the smaller religious group shows a true respect for their members' beliefs.

■ SEXUALITY

Although the Federal Fair Housing Act lists sex as a protected class, that only refers to discrimination based on whether male or female. There is no federal legislation that addresses sexual orientation. However, many states and local jurisdictions have provided protection from discrimination against gays and lesbians. The law itself changes very slowly; public perceptions often change even slower. This important segment of our population both needs and deserves special attention and presents another opportunity for a very special niche.

Here are a few more rather unusual niches described by the niche marketers themselves.

■ MILITARY RELOCATION

IN REAL LIFE | Ann Palmateer

Since our company is located in a predominantly military area with numerous bases that represent all the services, we decided to form a group of agents to target the military population for sales and rentals. In 1993, the company created a position of Military Relocation Director. They asked me, the wife of a Marine pilot for 28 years and a veteran of many moves, to take the position.

The reason for having military members on the team is that they are familiar with how the military sets up a move, how it takes place (different from corporate moves), the timing of orders, and the military pay scale. The mission of the team was to assist active-duty or retired military moving in and out of our area, making that a more pleasurable move with less stress. We developed extensive relocation packets geared to the military, mailing them to the personnel ahead of their transfer. We also regularly left information at the local bases' housing offices, and we set up plans to contact and visit bases outside our market where military would likely transfer from. We did a lot of research.

Initially I was paid a salary to market my company to the bases. I made regular visits to all ten local bases, leaving company information on how we could help their move. Eventually I branched out to visit bases on the West and East coasts. It was difficult to get my foot in those doors. What did help in getting in the door was that I had a military ID card and could talk the talk with the housing staff. Frequently, I took my husband with me, and that helped immensely. The important thing to remember is to reach your target before they come to town where they may make contact with other agents.

The military niche is in many respects unique and it varies from one location to another, depending on the attitude of the housing staff and their commanding officer. Often they don't realize that we are not competing with their staff, but that we can enhance their jobs by providing necessary information to their people so they can make intelligent decisions about their housing needs.

Many bases require their personnel to live on base, which also affects the market. Deployments also make it a tough decision for the military as to whether to buy or not. Some transfers to an area are joyous ones, while others are not happy moves. The agents must know the difference in order to assist the transferee. Many military also don't realize that they can buy instead of rent; education is thus a key factor. Many of the younger military have spent their pay on cars, motorcycles, and boats, and have several children, causing financial distress, so they need debt management counseling.

Making the military niche work requires research on the area, the housing available on base, and understanding the military move. The military niche marketer should have an ID card, as visiting bases is more difficult now because of tightened security. See what other companies in your area are doing. Visit the base, if you can, and find out how helpful their housing office might be. Also determine how you will reach personnel before they arrive in your market area. Plan your budget. This can be a very rewarding segment; once you break into a section or unit, they will recommend you to others.

■ INTERNATIONAL CLIENTS

IN REAL LIFE | **Angela Eliopoulos**

I have lived and worked in five different countries and feel like a global citizen myself. Living in an area like Washington, D.C., I constantly hear of clients needing to buy and sell properties not only locally but also abroad (such as summer homes or family estates), and I thought I might be able to assist them on both sides of the Atlantic.

I got my CIPS designation (Certified International Property Specialist) in 2000 and have also been active with FIABCI (International Real Estate Federation) since then. Networking with other international brokers is the most important aspect of our business. I also have an office in Athens, from where I cover all European Union countries. My recent sales have been in Paris, London, and the Ionian Islands, near Italy. If you visit our Web site at www.globalowner.com, you will be able to see some private islands and castles listed for sale.

I find my most effective marketing to be talking about what I do and advertising my services in the appropriate media. I recently had a client who lived in D.C. and needed to sell his home in Frankfurt in order to move up to a better home in D.C. Another special call was from a European property owner who had had his property listed with a well-known boutique international real estate company, but he decided he wanted more personal service. Although I was a little nervous considering the size of his previous listing company, I considered his call to be a great compliment. And I did get an offer shortly after receiving the listing!

■ THE CASINO!

IN REAL LIFE | Merry and Tom Cassabria

Our special niche involves Asian clients. I spent 15 years in the casino industry, and Tom is working on year 23. The casino industry employs many people whose first language is not English; employees can earn a decent wage and not be required to speak the language fluently. Because of this, we spent many years working alongside or supervising people of different cultures. We are interested in other cultures and very comfortable with people of other nationalities. They feel this, and are very comfortable with us as well.

When we moved to Connecticut, Tom's primary job was at the casino. He started working in real estate, and I followed a year later. Most of our Asian clients were from the casino. Tom would talk with them and tell them about the real estate market. One of our good friends, who is Asian, also moved to Connecticut at the same time. She spread the word among the Asian employees to use Tom and me as their REALTORS®. She is now our main translator. When we take our Asian clients out looking for houses, they are very comfortable with us, and we have developed a strong trust with them. They may not always understand what we are saying, but they know whatever we say is honest, and that we will always stand behind them. Tom also knows many phrases in various Asian languages, such as "Hi, how are you?", and "Are you feeling well?" This also helps break the ice with the newer clients.

So, we just fell into this Asian niche. One client kept referring another one, and so on. Our Asian business, which is about 2/3 of our total business, is no longer based entirely on casino acquaintances. However, many of the Asian buyers do move into this area to work at the casinos. We do no special marketing to our Asian clients; it is strictly word of mouth. Many times we have received messages in Chinese on our voice mail, but have no idea who it is or what they are saying. Because most of our Asian buyers speak little or no English at all, we rely extensively on our translators.

Once I tried to explain something to a new client who spoke decent English. Her friend, who had referred her to me, was there as well. The friend, a previous client, said something to the buyer in Chinese, and they both laughed. The friend then turned to me and said, "I told her she'll never understand everything, so just shut up and do whatever you tell her." It was funny, but she had said it because she trusts us. We find that once our Asian clients come to trust us, they trust us forever, and will always refer us.

Although we really enjoy working with our Asians buyers, we always know it's work. They are very tough negotiators, and make us earn our money! What we probably like best about working with our niche is that they never forget us. We are always getting Chinese food, candy, and other gifts dropped off to us. We have attended many parties where we are the only ones who speak fluent English, and they always invite our children as well.

Merry and Tom's experience is a perfect illustration of finding your niche right where you are. Try analyzing your present client base. You may find that you are in fact working a niche market whether that was your original intent or not. It is only natural to work with those with whom we live, work, or play. Determining your niche may be as simple as simply enlarging upon the client base that you already have. Honest answers to the following questions should help guide you to a niche group that you can be comfortable with and one where you can make a significant contribution to members of the niche.

- What's special about me?

- What unique skills do I have that could be helpful to others?

- What do I most enjoy doing?

- What area would I like to become an expert in?

- Which of my present clients do I most enjoy being with?

■ CONCLUSION

Almost everyone can sing, but very few make it to the Metropolitan Opera. Millions of youngsters play football but only a handful ever play in the Super Bowl. The chief difference between excellence and superiority is often due simply to a single factor: passion. To reach your own personal best, you must have a passion for what you are doing. Take time to develop the niche that is perfect for you—one that you can be passionate about serving—and begin to realize the financial power of niche marketing.

■ STEPS TO NICHE MARKETING SUCCESS

Identifying Your Niche

1. List all the spiritual, social, business, hobby, political, sports, and nonprofit organizations you belong to. List all the spiritual, social, business, hobby, political, sports and nonprofit organizations your spouse or partner belongs to.

2. List all the spiritual, social, business, hobby, political, sports, and nonprofit organizations your *children or relatives* belong to. List all the spiritual, social, business, hobby, political, sports, and nonprofit organizations your closest friends belong to.

3. List recurring groups, themes, or interests within these spiritual, social, business, hobby, political, sports, and nonprofit organizations.

4. List groups, themes, or interests you have always had an interest in.

5. List several issues, niches, or specific causes that you feel deeply about.

6. How many other agents in your area market to these specific issues, causes, or niches?

7. Gather marketing pieces from the agents targeting these issues, causes, or niches.

8. Review these marketing pieces.

9. Test market to two of your niches for one year.

10. Review your results after one year. Make revisions, additions, or deletions as you develop your next year's marketing plans.

5

Pursuing Your Niche

The first item on any to-do list after you define and decide to market to a niche group is to develop a business plan. Just as we define possible buyer profiles for our listing clients, we must do the same for our niche market. Ingredients for the niche profile can include overall niche demographics, income levels, first-time or move-up clients, and housing purchase/sale cycle in years (do owners tend to stay put, move up, or relocate). What do we know about their affinity for the niche; are they core, peripheral, or in between? Is their association with the niche based on political motivation, defined by the niche, or just an association that affirms their niche membership? How do niche members interact: through organized meetings, informal social gatherings, or in a more detached manner, such as by direct mail or e-mail?

Understanding how your niche members network will help you market to and network with them.

■ DEVELOPING A BUSINESS PLAN

How often have you heard someone say, "I just don't understand why I failed; everyone told me I had such a good idea." Unfortunately, good ideas are never more than a dream unless we make them a reality by starting with a solid business plan. We could write another whole book on effective business planning, but we will map out some of the basic elements here.

There are four distinct phases to business planning:

1. Research

All the great ideas in the world about working with immigrants won't amount to the proverbial hill of beans unless there actually are a large number of immigrants relocating in your area.

Larry Romito's example of working with single moms was based on demographic research that showed an unusually large number of single working mothers in that area. A tremendous program specially designed for senior clients won't go very far if you are located in an urban area of young singles. Do your homework first. It may be the most productive time you will spend on determining your niche market.

2. Develop a Plan

This is the heart of the project: a systematic outline of *what* you plan to do, *when* you plan to do it, and *how* you plan to do it. You already have your "great idea"—your dream. How can you make it work? It all comes down to goal setting.

Everyone has heard at least one talk on goal setting. We always resolve to do a better job. As with most goals, however, this great resolve usually fades away over time. We attend the lecture, take copious notes, and learn that goals must be specific, realistic, obtainable, and measurable.

A goal is seldom achieved unless you take the time to prepare an action plan complete with minor details. An action plan includes a step-by-step layout of what actually must be accomplished, who will be responsible for doing the work and—most important—what is the deadline for completion of each action. Last of all—but in no way the least—are the details. Specific detail planning is what makes it possible to carry out the actions in a timely way. Look at the sample action plan below to see how precise the details are. Nit-picky? Maybe, but this is what makes it all work.

3. Carry Out Your Plan

Just do it!!

4. Evaluate Your Plan

The last phase of business planning is absolutely essential. Take time to regularly check on your progress. You will need to stop regularly for a reality check; these checkpoints should never be more than three months apart. Is the plan working? Are deadlines for actions being met? If not, perhaps some changes or adjustments need to be made. Another reason many great ideas fail is that the goals are often set unrealistically. When it becomes apparent after a few months that these unrealistic goals are not being met, the whole idea is simply dropped. A much better approach is to reevaluate the plan. The basic idea may be fine; it just needs more tweaking of the action plan and details.

■ DEVELOPING A MARKETING PLAN

Have you ever sat in a brainstorming session on how to develop a better marketing plan for your company? Great ideas are flying everywhere. Everyone leaves the meeting enthused and excited about the new direction the company will be taking and how much more successful everyone will be. A month later at the next planning meeting, you wonder what has happened. Probably nothing. Those great ideas have to be turned into goals. Each goal must be developed into a strong action plan. Every action must be broken down into details—specific details outlining who is responsible and when it must be completed. When you are pursuing your new niche market, you may be the only one responsible for all four steps in developing your plan; however, you still need to set deadlines for yourself. The extra hours spent in research and good business planning are the best hours you can ever spend in pursuing your niche market and increasing your overall production. See the table below for an example of how to prepare a good action plan.

■ SAMPLE ACTION PLAN

GOAL: Develop a Seniors Niche Market

ACTION 1: Research the demographics in my area.

DETAILS:	What	When
	1. Check census.gov on Internet	next 2 days
	2 Check city Web site on Internet	next 2 days
	3. Visit city planning office: meet with Jack Jones at 4:00 on Wednesday	midweek
	4. Pull up city tax records to locate long-term owners	by end of week

ACTION 2: Prepare initial mailing into neighborhoods with seniors.

DETAILS:	What	When
	1. Select neighborhoods for mailing (3)	end of week 2
	2. Write letter for mailing	midweek 2
	3. Collect names & addresses for mailing	end of week 2
	4. Compare cost of mailing service vs. doing myself (choose mailing service)	end of week 2

ACTION 3: Develop follow-up plan for monthly contact.

DETAILS:	What	When
	1. Research available "canned" programs	end of week 4
	2. Read books, articles on working with seniors to pick best methods of communication	end of week 4
	3. Lay out specific program for contacts (phone calls, mailings, visits)	end of week 5
	4. Set up system for record keeping for each household contact	end of week 5

■ GETTING ORGANIZED

Organization is unquestionably an essential business tool. Many excellent books are available on business planning and time management. Every one of them stresses the importance of writing out your plan and making lists. Making lists is one of the most effective ways to manage processes and set priorities. Part of good business planning is to set goals with monthly, quarterly, and annual benchmarks. After setting and achieving some small goals, you will find yourself motivated to set larger ones as you become more confident in your ability to meet them.

Regularly conduct an honest analysis of your plan and your goals to determine if you need to make corrections or alterations, or possibly even to terminate your plan to market to a specific niche group. Many factors come into business planning, and real estate selling has both macro and micro market-driven variables that could have an impact on your niche marketing business plan.

You should probably experiment with various media options, including different types of print media, as well as radio and cable TV. For some niche groups an effective Web site and e-mail may give you the best results. As your niche market develops, you will likely find that word of mouth is absolutely the best way to reach your niche community. Whichever style of marketing you choose, however, always be sure you are up-to-date on current real estate consumer trends in your market area. Talk regularly to members of your niche, asking for feedback. Evaluating their responses will help you decide when to shift your marketing budget from one medium to another.

■ LOYALTY

Client loyalty is difficult to earn for any real estate professional. Ideally we would all like to become that client's "REALTOR® for Life." However, surveys have shown that although immediately after closing 98 percent of the clients say they would use the same agent again, in reality only slightly over 10 percent do. Managing brokers can tell you why this happens: *lack of follow-up!* In many ways, client loyalty may be easier to achieve in working a niche market. These are clients who already have a basis of commonality with their agent. Because these agents are working in an area for which they have a passion, there is a much higher likelihood that they will stay in touch—just because they want to.

IN REAL LIFE | Mark Nash

In my niche marketing to the gay and lesbian segment, I have heard many times from other experienced agents in my office how loyal this niche is. Generally, they have been more loyal than my non-niche clients, but I believe that loyalty in real estate sales is based more on the agent's business style and ethics. Most of my niche clients are loyal because of our commonality and my business style. They have told me that I provide a higher level of comfort with my understanding and affirmation of their profile.

Can non-niche agents provide this? I'm sure that in many communities they do. However, they sometimes may make insensitive comments. This is probably more out of a lack of knowledge than any prejudice, but it does affect the relationship with the client. Respect for the members of the niche and understanding their unique dynamic are the most important rules for earning and keeping their respect and business. Most people are sensitive to patronizing behavior and do not react to it positively.

■ DOES NICHE MARKETING ENTAIL STEERING?

If you were not already familiar with particular niche groups in your market area, you probably will become more aware after being in real estate even for a relatively short time. You may encounter clients who are members of a particular niche and realize that you will not be able to provide the type of quality service that they deserve. Consider referring them to a real estate professional who does specialize in working with that particular group. Fair housing laws require that we treat all potential clients and customers equally, without discrimination against any of the classes protected by federal, state, or local regulations classes. There is no restriction, however, on assisting consumers by providing them with an agent who will give them better guidance and more effective service. The key here is to make it possible for the prospect to connect with someone who will be best able to help them achieve their goal of either buying or selling real estate. Under no circumstances should any person be denied the opportunity to realize their real estate goals. Equally important is that no agent should ever be guilty of steering clients either toward or away from any given property based on their race, color, religion, national origin, gender, familial status, or any mental or physical handicap.

■ CREATING UNIQUENESS

All marketers of products and services search for ways to make their product unique, because that is what the consumer typically identifies with. Consumer products claim to be "the biggest," "the brightest," "the longest-lasting," or "the best bargain." People buy the product because they want to identify with the claims. In the real estate business we basically do the same thing. An agent may claim to be "the expert on FHA foreclosures," "the specialist in Internet marketing," "the most knowledgeable buyer agent." We want people to come to us because they want the unique aspect of real estate practice that we have to offer. In many cases you may be able to promote your unique claim to fame based on your past experience in the business world. For example, Mike had been a loan officer and decided to switch over to the selling side of the business. Because of his knowledge about the many loan products that are

IN REAL LIFE | Mark Nash

When I first started my business plan to reach the gay and lesbian market, I was aware of other agents who were already marketing to the *urban* subniche within the larger overall metropolitan community. So the first light bulb that went off was to pursue the *suburban* gay and lesbian subniche and their need for a niche-sensitive real estate sales agent. After completing some research on how other suburban agents were marketing to the niche, I discovered that they were not very assertive in their pursuit. My first foundation-laying exercise in pursuing my niche was to start to increase my name visibility within the gay and lesbian community. Name visibility and affiliation with my brokerage firm helped provide the foundation, but helping the community on whatever level they needed was the mortar for building on that.

especially geared to the first-time homebuyer, this became his niche. His advertising described himself as "Your financial expert—call me and learn how you can buy your first home today!" He was selling his expertise. This made him unique in the eyes of potential clients. He had another ad: "Tired of renting? Let me show you how you could own your own home in just 30 days!" Another ad promoting zero-money-down options read: "No cash? No worry! No-money-down loans are available today for first-time homebuyers!" His aggressive advertising brought in the calls.

IN REAL LIFE | Doris Barrell

I once had clients who had to make a very quick move due to job changes and other crazy circumstances. As a result I had to go to settlement for them with power of attorney for the sale of their house in Alexandria. This solved the settlement problem, but the greater issue was their two cats. The family had already moved to Raleigh, N.C. The cats had been in a kennel in Alexandria for two weeks, but now they needed transport to Raleigh. As it happens, I do love cats and was very fond of my clients. So, I loaded up my car with the two cat carriers, the litter box, and treats for the road and off we went—Paws, Chita, and me for the five-hour drive to Raleigh. Unique service—definitely. A little crazy—probably. Value perception—priceless! Do you think they became raving fans? Absolutely!

■ VALUE PERCEPTIONS

Perceptions, good or bad, make or break any business. We know that word of mouth is always the best kind of advertising. However, it can also cause the most damage. Unfortunately, people often remember the bad longer than they do the good. Psychological studies show that a roomful of positive thinkers will still have trouble overcoming one person with a negative outlook. Look at the front page of your newspaper. Bad news, disaster, tragedy—that sells newspapers. People love to share their experiences, and a bad one usually makes for a better story. Anyone who provides a service to the public knows that you can't please everyone. No matter how well you do or how hard you try, there will always be some people who think you did a poor job, or who just plain don't like you. As a popular nationally known real estate instructor once said, "If you don't like your client, there's a real good chance he doesn't like you either."

In our niche market, we do try even harder to please them all. Because the whole niche market concept is based on relationships and unique service, we do have a better chance at creating this perception of extra value. Ken Blanchard, author of *One-Minute Manager*, wrote another book called *Raving Fans*. Every niche marketer should read this book and incorporate Blanchard's basic premise of giving the client 100 percent service plus one! As he says, "Meet their expectations and then surpass them."

IN REAL LIFE | Mark Nash

When I began marketing to the suburban gay and lesbian community, part of my business plan was to have a slow entry, gradual build-up, and a long-term plateau. In the beginning of my marketing program, I had a distinct non-sales approach. Most of my cold-calling focused on bridging the large geographically based community. People gradually became aware that I was interested in more than my next commission check. They realized that I had a perception of value in the community and that I wasn't just involved to necessarily make a quick monetary gain from them. After creating a value perception of being affirming to the niche, my next value issue was in the transaction itself. Being professional, accessible, and ethical were the chief additional principles of value that I brought to the transaction. Receiving value is a winner every time with real estate sales clients!

Each year a Gallup Poll survey ranks about fifty professions for ethical reputation. All too often, the consumer thinks of real estate agents as being located very near the bottom of the list. In fact, each year real estate agents have reached a slightly higher standing. Hopefully, we can continue to change this negative perception as we earn loyalty from our niche customers and clients.

■ CREATING AWARENESS

In long-term business planning, you have to start with one idea and slowly add additional points to be successful in a niche. Don't spread yourself too thin. Remember that it is *long-term* planning; you cannot expect to see results overnight.

As part of your business plan, consider incorporating the goal of creating awareness of your uniqueness niche through your relationships with other organizations. The National Association of REALTORS® has a program called "Good Neighbor Awards." REALTORS® throughout the country are recognized for their contributions to the communities in which they live and work. In some cases the REALTOR® may have worked with an organization like Habitat for Humanity or Boy Scouts of America. In one case the agent promised a group of first graders that she would send them to college if they just stayed in school. Most of them did, and she made good on her promise! Each award winner has a different story, but the essence is the same. These sales professionals are giving back to their community, not for their own glory and not as a marketing tool, but out of a true sense of caring. An old adage states, "No one cares how much you know until they know how much you care." True caring is recognized and appreciated. It follows naturally that people receiving your care will now be interested in your knowledge and will become loyal members of your niche group.

IN REAL LIFE | Mark Nash

Early in my career, I began forming relationships with several different organizations. Where I found receptiveness, I tried helping them meet their needs—and they all had many! At first I offered mainly publicity for the organizations in my monthly newsletter for the community. Eventually I made contributions to or sponsored fund-raising functions for various organizations. I was careful to be diplomatic with my resources to avoid alienating subniches. After about one year I became one of several spokespersons for the suburban gay and lesbian community. Included with each published quote was my name and my brokerage company's name. I wanted readers and listeners to fill in the blanks and think to themselves that they could have an affirming REALTOR® who was sensitive to the gay and lesbian community and who also knew their geography. Realizing that I was going to support the suburban Chicago gay and lesbian community in my real estate sales business, I first had to affirm and support them before loyalty and business was returned. My intent was to build long-term foundations in the niche.

Because the suburban community was detached geographically from the urban community, it had unique needs and dynamics. I started to build affirming, supportive relationships with suburban-based gay and lesbian organizations. Soon I realized that not only were the suburban communities isolated from the urban community, they were also isolated from each other. Overcoming the isolation became the drive behind my efforts to build relationships and give back to the suburban community while developing a growing awareness of my real estate sales business.

IN REAL LIFE | Mark Nash

Early in developing my niche market, I realized that one of the common needs of the suburban gay and lesbian community was a need for a gathering of all the groups, organizations, and subniches. These groups were spread over a large geographic area; I thought a business and resource expo comprising gay and lesbian businesses and resources (and businesses friendly to them) would help unite this diverse and historically difficult to reach demographic. I also thought this would help illustrate the size of the demographic to future marketers to this community. Nonprofit organizations serving the suburban community later provided me with another way to give back various resources I had to support their mission. Being a board member of nonprofit organizations also created exposure for my real estate sales business as well as giving back to the community.

My niche advertising budget was never large enough for all the requests for sponsorship I received from organizations in the suburban gay and lesbian community. One area of no-cost advertising available to me was the gay and lesbian Chicago weekly newspapers. After listing ads in them, I pursued the editorial staffs to allow me to be quoted on real estate issues in the suburbs. Several stories appeared with quotes from me on market conditions in my geographical area. These stories led to a *Chicago Tribune* story on Gay Pride Weekend, where I was photographed and quoted as Evanston REALTOR® Mark Nash. At the same time Chicago-based LesBiGay Radio had established a large suburban following. The station owner was on my relationship list and a real estate client. I started to sponsor shows

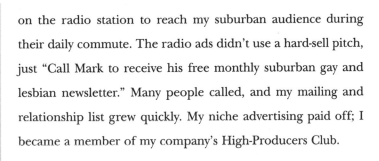

on the radio station to reach my suburban audience during their daily commute. The radio ads didn't use a hard-sell pitch, just "Call Mark to receive his free monthly suburban gay and lesbian newsletter." Many people called, and my mailing and relationship list grew quickly. My niche advertising paid off; I became a member of my company's High-Producers Club.

◼ GIVING BACK

Niche segments are sensitive to the motivations of businesses that market to them. It is always wise to first find ways to contribute and develop a sincere interest in the niche group before looking for reciprocity from the niche members in your real estate sales business. Building relationships is the foundation of niche marketing. Of course we are in business to make money; that's what business is all about. We must, however, also be in the niche marketing business to provide unique service to a special group of clients. Giving back to the niche market community is not only a way to pursue a new niche market but also a vital part of continuing those relationships.

◼ FOCUSING

You must stay focused on only one or two niche groups. Marketing to niches can be time-intensive; to reap a return from niche marketing, you cannot simply add another relationship "farm" to your real estate sales business. Pursuing a niche is not a decision to make lightly, as it requires time, resources, and loyalty from you to receive business down the road. If you have selected a niche that seems too large for you to handle, consider a subniche. After spending some time working with a sub-niche, you may feel a need to become even more focused on distinct elements of the niche (see examples).

Example:
Original niche: First-time home buyers
Subniche: First-time home buyers interested in buying distressed properties
Sub-subniche: First-time home buyers interested in buying FHA foreclosures

Example:
Original niche: Seniors
Subniche: Baby boomers
Sub-subniche: Baby boomers interested in golf, ski, or fishing resort second homes

Example:
Original niche: Hispanic immigrants
Subniche: Latin American Hispanic immigrants
Sub-subniche: El Salvadorian Hispanic immigrants

Example:
Original niche: Gay and lesbian suburban real estate consumers
Subniche: North and Northwest suburban gay and lesbian real estate consumers
Sub-subniche: North and Northwest suburban gay and lesbian first-time home buyers

■ CONCLUSION

Niche marketing is a proactive real estate sales business tool. It is not unlike traditional farming, in that it has a delayed response time and is related to the time, sincerity, and resource you have devoted to it. You are actually building a sub-business within your main real estate sales business. To build this sub-business, you need to lay a foundation and, as you continue building relationships, wait for the eventual response. Niche marketing is not for agents who want immediate sales response. It is for those who enjoy deriving some nonfinancial compensation in addition to commissions, rewards that come from helping a niche grow, evolve, and prosper. We cannot begin to describe all the positive business and personal benefits that can be received from niche marketing over the years. We strongly believe in it; we have found that it has treated us well in our personal real estate sales business and brought us great personal satisfaction.

■ STEPS TO NICHE MARKETING SUCCESS

1. Calculate your budget for year-one marketing to each of your two niches.

2. Calculate your time allocation for year one to each of your two niches.

3. List four ways you will add uniqueness to each niche.

4. List three ways you will build loyalty from each niche to yourself.

5. List three ways you will demonstrate your loyalty to each niche.

6. List three ways you will give your resources back to each niche.

7. List your marketing and time commitment to each niche by each month, quarter, and year.

8. List your long-range plans for years two and three to further develop and expand your niche presence.

9. List what you personally and professionally plan to receive from your niches.

10. Take all of the ideas listed above and incorporate them into a written business plan, complete with an action plan full of details. Remember to reevaluate your plan regularly—at least every three months.

6 Building Your Niche

In earlier chapters we have spoken at length about the different types of niche markets and given suggestions on how to select a niche market that is best suited to your own interests. Now let us look at some ways to continue building that niche beyond the original member group.

■ PRINT ADVERTISING

The real estate business spends an enormous amount of money each year on newspaper ads. Some special ways of using this type of advertising can be effective in spreading the word about your new niche market specialty. In many cities there are local newspapers published in the languages of various ethnic groups within the community. For example, in the Mount Vernon area of Alexandria, Virginia, there is a large Korean community. An agent who decided to specialize in this group began to run ads in the Korean newspaper. (Be careful to also run ads in the local English-speaking newspaper in order to avoid the implication of steering, which would be a fair housing violation.)

In the Annandale area of northern Virginia there is a strong Asian community with large groups of Vietnamese and Chinese. Some stores in that area cater especially to people from those communities. One agent had an excellent idea for promoting business among the Vietnamese. He prepared a flyer about himself and his services in Vietnamese, then had copies printed at a local quick-print shop operated by a Vietnamese man. Next he requested permission to leave stacks of the flyers at the print shop, the adjoining grocery and sundries shop, the barber shop, and the dry-cleaning shop. This was an effective promotional idea to seek new clients.

A local newspaper is another effective way to increase your niche presence. Volunteer to provide a weekly column on real estate issues, perhaps using "Ask Bob" type of question-and-answer format.

■ WEB SITES AND THE INTERNET

The use of the Internet in real estate sales is here to stay. You should keep in mind several fundamentals about Internet consumers. First, they like the anonymity that protects them from unwanted interaction. Second, they like to be in control of communication and keep it impersonal. Third, they appreciate that the Internet gives them information that helps them make a more educated, decision which results in more efficient shopping.

There are three different types of Web sites to consider. On each of these sites, include as much information as you can about yourself, your business, and your expertise in your special niche market.

Realtor.com

This is a national Web site for real estate listings and real estate sales agents that receives information through the brokers. You can purchase your own personal Web page on this site so that clients shopping for a real estate sales agent in your market can find you. You can also choose from other national Web sites.

Your company Web site

Make sure that your current agent profile, your e-mail address, and your telephone extension or direct line are on your agent page. This enables the prospect to find you, not just your company.

Your own Web site

Many agents today have their own personal Web sites. Recent NAR reports show that practitioners with a personal Web site earn about twice as much as those without one. A Web site can be set up at a relatively low cost for someone who is computer literate or can be provided by various professional services. Once it is set up, it can move with you if you should change broker affiliation or geographic area.

You should develop content for your personal Web site that provides information and resources for your potential clients. Have your Web site "seeded" (the tech word for *listed*) in the top search engines and enjoy 24/7 advertising for your own real estate sales business. Most Web site developers are technology based. Consider having the graphic design for your site created by a visual designer. An on-line brochure without interesting content and visual appeal will not attract potential clients; be sure to think it through carefully. Visit Web sites on-line to get a feel for what the public is viewing at other Web sites, then make yours even better! Remember to include testimonials from clients and feature your own current listings.

Computer marketing can be especially appealing to baby boomers and generation Xers. Young people today have grown up with computers and use them daily in both their work and their personal lives. Most of their information in a broad range of areas comes from the Internet.

Web site Content Ideas

- About you: Your real estate professional profile

- Contact information for you: E-mail address and link, phone numbers, fax numbers, and brokerage name and address

- Information of interest to your chosen niche market

- Your current listings

- List of areas or communities you serve

- Testimonials from active or sold clients

- Your market's weather information, including monthly highs and lows

- School information for your market

- A simple sign-up process to be on your mailing list

- Links to home-finding sites (Realtor.com, local MLS, etc.)

- Process used in selling a home in your market

- Process used in purchasing a home in your market

- Relocation information specific to your market

- MapQuest link, so the geography of your market can be visualized

- Site map

- Community information

- Sports activities, cultural events, tourist information—whatever you think will attract their interest

IN REAL LIFE | Mark Nash

Outrealty.com was my technology advertising to reach the gay and lesbian real estate consumer. Early Internet user demographics illustrated a larger-than-average gay and lesbian user base. Many speculated the anonymity of that medium allowed the community to seek out information about the community in a more private format. Applying my successful relationship-based marketing to the Internet, I designed my Web site to focus on gay and lesbian resources with a low-key pitch for my real estate sales business. E-mails began arriving quickly and consistently—numerous requests for my services or referrals to other gays and lesbians in the Chicago area and nationwide. This illustrates the enormous audience for niche-specific real estate Internet sites. The Internet business helped drive my sales volume to Prudential Properties' President's Circle Level: the top 5% of all Prudential sales agents in the nation.

■ MAILINGS AND NEWSLETTERS

Regular mailings have always been an important marketing tool for any agent farming a particular area. These can also be an effective tool in niche marketing, but only if the mailing is specific to the particular niche. The cute recipe cards that have been around for years might be meaningless to someone from a different culture. On the other hand, a regular newsletter with news items from within a specific ethnic community might be well received. Refrigerator magnet calendars have always been popular, but a list of emergency phone numbers would be more helpful to someone with limited English. The senior client niche group may find it especially helpful to receive news items about changes in the tax laws applying to selling property or changes in the estate tax laws that could affect them or their heirs. Monthly newsletters have a definite place in a marketing strategy, but they must be oriented toward the special needs and interests of your niche group—never a type of canned offerings that can be ordered from a catalog and sent out by bulk mail.

■ BUSINESS AND OTHER ORGANIZATIONS

Rotary Club, the Elks, Kiwanis, and other community-oriented groups have traditionally served as good networking sources. Do research to locate groups more specific to your niche market. There may be business organizations that specialize in a particular ethic group or nationality. Occasionally, a local Chamber of Commerce will have special branches or committees that concentrate on a particular subpopulation of the city.

IN REAL LIFE | **Mark Nash**

One of the first steps in my action plan was to begin compiling a mailing list from friends and gay and lesbian directories. Soon I had a sufficient list to send out my first monthly newsletter: the *Nash Report.* It comprised specific suburban community information pertaining to housing, schools, transportation, and so on. Also included were gay and lesbian resources, organizations, and business information, focusing on the Chicago suburbs, as well as articles on home improvement, mortgage rates, and gay and lesbian relocation. The newsletter was a resource for the readers; it had a minimal sales pitch for my real estate sales business. After a couple of months of publication, people began calling to get on the mailing list or to request that I write about their organization. I received many referrals from direct or pass-along readers of the *Nash Report.*

■ RELIGIOUS ORGANIZATIONS

Religious affiliations are very important in some societies. In fact, the majority of United States citizens describe themselves as belonging to some religious group. Many niches exist, for example, Catholic, Lutheran, Evangelical, Protestant, Jewish, Islamic. Most of these niches have subniches. You must to take time learn about the primary religions of those in your niche market. Many agents have seriously offended Muslim clients by setting up business appointments on a Friday during their normal worship period. There are Buddhist temples in many metropolitan areas. If you are ever fortunate enough to be invited to a Buddhist wedding or funeral ceremony, be prepared as to what to expect. Do not plan on a 15-minute ceremony followed by an hour reception in the church hall. And even the most westernized of Eastern clients often rely on their cultural heritage for such rites of passage as birth, marriage, and death.

■ CULTURAL EVENTS

Becoming aware of special occasions and participating in them can be among the most enjoyable parts of working within a niche market. Every culture has its own special days for celebration, and your clients will be thrilled that you care to learn about them and share these experiences with them.

For example, large communities of Mexicans are located throughout the country. Their Cinco de Mayo celebrations may last far longer than the "fifth of May!" Another important day in the life of some Hispanic girls is their 15th birthday—*la quinceaños*. Smart agents working with any of the various Hispanic groups will find that special occasion cards in Spanish provide a pleasant surprise for their clients.

If you are considering working with Hispanics, you must focus on only one—or perhaps two—specific subgroups within that enormous population. People from many different countries speak some form of Spanish. You must be aware of each group's unique customs, needs, and interests.

■ COMMUNITY EVENTS

In addition to cultural or ethnic festivals every year, a multitude of civic or community events also provide an opportunity for networking and expanding your niche. An agent who specialized in working with the families of firefighters always had an active presence in the fire department's annual open house

IN REAL LIFE | **Doris Barrell**

At one time, I managed a small office in a section of Alexandria that had a fast-growing population of immigrants from El Salvador. Their customs, their food, and even their pronunciations in Spanish were very different from those of my Spanish-speaking agent from Puerto Rico. It would be like comparing someone from Scotland with someone from Texas! Same language, but entirely different niche groups. Determine which particular Hispanic group has the most interest for you, then concentrate on learning everything you can about that group.

program. Holding a booth at the county fair, community flea market, or urban block party is another way to let the community know who you are and what you represent.

■ CHARITY AND OTHER NONPROFIT ORGANIZATIONS

Some agents will say "Oh, I can't work with people from my church. They would think I was taking advantage of them!" Whether it is your church group or another charity or nonprofit group of which you are a part, there is certainly nothing wrong with being available to provide real estate services to members of that group. Whom would they more likely trust—you, someone they know and work with, or a complete stranger whom they located by calling a real estate office? No agents want to appear crass or self-serving by overpromoting themselves, but it is certainly acceptable for you to make sure that members of the organization are aware that you are a real estate professional and you would enjoy helping them meet their needs and wants.

Every charity or nonprofit that we know of has two consistent needs: more volunteers and more money! You can provide time and energy as a volunteer. You can also help by using your marketing skills to help the organization promote itself through fund-raising activities.

■ BUILDING A TEAM FOR YOUR NICHE

Other professionals, such as attorneys, are important in providing service for our niche market members. Understanding the legal aspects of a real estate transaction is no easy task even for those born and raised in the U.S. Imagine trying to understand all this in some other language. People prefer to do business in a language that they understand and with people who understand their needs. While everyone has to conduct their real estate business in the U.S. according to its federal and state laws, there is nothing wrong with having someone help you interpret those laws in a language that you understand.

If you specialize in an ethnic or national niche market but do not speak the language of that group, you will need to seek help. You must develop a team of professionals who will be able to meet the needs of clients with limited English. Many U.S. attorneys and settlement agents today are able and willing to conduct settlements in Spanish, Chinese, Vietnamese, and other languages.

Other professional members of your team may include an attorney specializing in elder law, a certified public accountant, a financial planner, and someone knowledgeable about estate tax, probate provisions, and the advantages and disadvantages of living trusts.

First-time home buyers need additional professional help in the areas of financing and settlement procedures. An attorney who can explain the various ways that title may be held to a property would be beneficial. Also, a lawyer may be needed to clarify laws regarding property rights when one partner dies intestate (without a will), which could present a problem for a gay or lesbian couple.

Each particular niche may require different areas of information to be covered by members of the niche marketer's team of professionals.

IN REAL LIFE | Doris Barrell

Neighborhood Reinvestment Corporation provides training throughout the country for nonprofit housing organizations. As a training consultant for them, I teach classes on residential financing and home-buyer education counseling. One of the suggestions that I often make is for the housing organization to invite a REALTOR® to attend their home-buyer education seminars to explain the home-buying process. In a way, these REALTORS® are developing a niche market for first-time home-buyers. The REALTOR® actually becomes a partner with the housing organization.

This niche does not appeal to everyone, since there are often many hours spent with a potential client that never result in a successful transaction. The financial problems may be overwhelming, or the prospective buyer's motivation to continue with the process may be lacking. REALTORS® who work in this niche often comment that the rewards they receive from helping people achieve their American dream of home ownership far outweigh any dollar amounts they might receive.

■ BUNDLING SERVICE PROVIDERS

Bundling transaction service providers who are affirming to your niche helps niche consumers feel comfortable with all aspects of their transaction. Service bundling is actually cross-referring to the members of your niche group. Mortgage brokers, attorneys, loan officers, and other professionals who are also members of the niche group may be able to overcome the inevitable problems that occur in real estate transactions.

■ CONCLUSION

Just as a brick house is built by starting with a strong foundation and then adding row after row of bricks, so will your niche market grow. After a certain amount of trial and error you will determine which of the print and other media best reach out to your niche members. Even more important will be your personal involvement in those business, cultural, and community organizations and events that are important to the people included in your selected niche. Start building your team of other service providers who understand the special needs of your particular niche members. Be involved, show that you care, and watch your niche market grow.

■ STEPS TO NICHE MARKETING SUCCESS

Building Your Niche

1. Choose one print medium to market to your niche.

2. Book a minimum of eight hits to your niche from your chosen print medium.

3. Have a Web site developed to market to your niche, reaching the invisible niche members.

4. Join at least two chambers of commerce, business organizations, or other associations related to your niche.

5. Attend at least seven events that are related to your niche.

6. Sponsor or have a business presence at two or more niche-related events.

7. Develop a list to telemarket or direct mail to other businesses related to or part of your niche.

7

Marketing and Beyond

Marketing is a long-term commitment for an agent in the niche real estate sales business. The goal is to achieve name recognition and a presence that causes people to think of you when they have any real estate needs. In this Chapter we will look at the elements of marketing that go beyond mere advertising, such as making use of your prior business skills and ways to brand yourself. The new niche marketer must be aware of the commitment involved in developing a niche market, the need to build confidence in the niche consumer, and the various ways to constantly reaffirm the members of the niche group.

Chapter Four described several different niche groups. In this Chapter we have developed a longer list of potential niches. Depending on your own background, interests, and abilities, you may come up with even more possibilities. Remember, any group of individuals who have a common core of interests, needs, and wants constitutes a niche. Your job is to build the niche group's confidence in you and your services and to continually reaffirm the members of the niche group.

■ EIGHT IS THE MAGIC NUMBER

The marketing industry has established that it takes eight hits on a consumer before they even remember your name. Plan on a minimum of eight ads—and probably four more before they are motivated to call *you*. Consumers are bombarded daily with so many advertisements that they have to first edit what comes in, then focus on what is relevant to their current needs. How many times have you thrown away flyers featuring bargain prices for new tires? You may not even think about it—until the day you have a blow-out on the way home. Then you start searching through the trash frantically looking for the ad.

■ PREPARE FOR A LONG-TERM COMMITMENT

Both traditional farming and niche marketing require a long-term commitment on the part of the agent. If it takes at least eight repetitions before anyone will even *recognize* your name, how long does it take to establish a relationship? Far too often, new agents start off highly enthusiastic about their new farm. They spend hours developing the mailing list, and dollars having introductory letters and monthly newsletters printed. They spend even more hours delivering the newsletters or walking the neighborhood to hand out goodies like calendars, sports schedules, or note pads. The agent may be bitterly disappointed if the phone does not ring off the hook after the first month or two of farming.

Whether geographic or niche, developing a special market takes time and patience. And it does cost money to market yourself. All agents should plan to spend at least ten percent of their income on marketing themselves. At first, that is all money going out with no return. However, the return from only *one* commission is usually enough to pay for almost one year's worth of personal marketing!

■ PRESELLING THROUGH RELATIONSHIP BUILDING

All sales agents hope that every one of their clients or customers will be pleased with their services and will cheerfully recommend them to others. This is one of the primary building blocks of establishing a client referral base. In many cases, however, the agent fails to follow up with the client after settlement, and the opportunity to build on that initial success is lost. Niche marketing emphasizes the importance of establishing good relationships as well as providing good service. This provides a stronger foundation on which to build a solid referral business. When one niche client recommends you to another member of the niche group, they have effectively presold both you and your services. This dramatically reduces the amount of time it will take you to convince the prospective client that you are the best person to help them achieve their needs.

Building Confidence in the Niche Consumer

We are here to be a resource and business professional to our clients. By being active listeners, as well as well-organized and proactive, we affirm our clients' decisions in their sale or purchase transaction. Being controlling or self-focused is not in the client's best interest or perceived as affirming to them. Once your clients have trust in your added value, you can make professional suggestions from your real estate sales experience.

IN REAL LIFE | Mark Nash

When my phone rings at the real estate sales office, it is typically from a referral—through a niche client, a business relationship or an agent.

The phone ringing today is often the result of many months and years of laying my niche-relationship–based business foundation. The niche caller on the other end of the phone has been presold my services by another member of the niche group.

Preselling is what has driven my real estate sales business and keeps my niche client pipeline flowing. If the niche referral is not in the position to use my services today, I try to extend an offer of other services available from members of my real estate relationship sphere. This leaves them with the feeling that I wasn't there just to derive an immediate benefit from them, but to assist them in whatever their immediate needs might be. This absolutely creates loyalty and continues to build new niche referrals.

Keep in mind that you have been retained to meet the clients' objectives and to affirm their decisions in the process. They can always choose a different real estate service professional if they don't feel confident with you.

One way to build confidence with the consumer is for you to show a genuine interest in what affects their lives, beyond the buying and selling of a property. All too often the public has the perception that real estate agents are just "in it for the bucks." Look for ways that you can contribute to the overall community and, of course, to your special niche.

IN REAL LIFE | **Mark Nash**

IN REAL LIFE | **Mark Nash**

After achieving a solid foundation in the real estate sales business, in part from the support of the suburban Chicago gay and lesbian community, I decided the next step in my business development was to give back to the community. Joining the board of the suburban Chicago-based nonprofit organization BE HIV (better existence with HIV) provided me with the opportunity to give back both my time and resources. My involvement with BE HIV also provided me with new relationships to build upon. I enjoyed networking at various fund-raising events, promoting the suburban community, and being involved with it through my real estate business.

More recently, the owner of LesBiGay Radio wanted to raise funds for his station. Knowing my nonprofit history and vast gay and lesbian relationship network, he asked if I would cochair a fundraiser with him for his nonprofit station. We built a successful event that brought in more donations than any other fundraiser the station had ever had. It was a great pleasure for me personally to donate my services as well as resources to his station.

■ LIFE BEFORE REAL ESTATE

You can often apply previous skills, learned in your life before real estate to developing your niche market practice. Combining good business skills and quality relationships leads to spin-off referral business generated from your initial contacts.

IN REAL LIFE | Doris Barrell

Although we didn't even know the term *niche* twenty years ago when I started in the real estate business, I now know that back then I actually was working a niche market. From the beginning of my career, I tended to work with first-time home buyers. I've always had a keen interest in mortgage financing and kept myself well informed on various programs for first-timers—mostly FHA in those days. All too often, these young people had been turned away by more experienced agents who didn't want to be bothered with their problems, doubts, lack of cash, and so on.

Since I was a brand-new agent with a great need for income and plenty of time (I was recently divorced and starting a whole new career), I was more than willing to take on the challenge. In the interest of finding buyers I volunteered for every minute of desk-duty floor time that was available. Many of these calls would be people just starting to think about buying a home for the first time. When we were successful in finding them a home that they could afford, they were ecstatic and, of course, told all their friends. That led to additional buyers who were already presold on the value of my services. As a side benefit, I also received business from some of the parents. I remember one mother telling me that every other agent had just shrugged off her daughter and son-in-law but I had taken the time to help them. She was so appreciative that she wanted to list her house with me.

IN REAL LIFE | Doris Barrell

The next step in developing my first-timer *niche* market involved selling my business skills rather than specific listings. Through a good friend who worked for a local attorney, I became very interested in the equity-sharing concept. In the early to mid-eighties we had many people wanting to invest in real estate. They were justifiably concerned about the problems connected with handling rental properties: how to find good tenants who were financially qualified, how well the tenants would maintain the property, and what to do if a tenant left without paying the rent.

I started holding public seminars on equity sharing and soon found that my first-time home-buyer niche group was a perfect match for my new niche group of persons interested in buying real estate as an investment. My colleagues began to call me the "Matchmaker Dolly" of real estate. I would find a property that fit the needs and wants of the first-timers, match them up with an investor, have the attorney prepare the agreement between the equity-sharing parties, present an offer on the property, secure the financing, and go to settlement with two sets of very satisfied clients.

In later years I often assisted the home buyers in buying out their investor partner or in listing and selling the property with profits distributed to both parties. Unfortunately, Tax Recovery Act of '86 (known in some circles as the Tax Disaster Act) put an abrupt end to the tax benefits achieved in this type of transaction, and my double-niche came tumbling down! However, this business was great while it lasted, and it brought me numerous loyal clients who continued to regard me as "their agent" in many subsequent transactions.

The majority of REALTORS® do not go directly from college into the real estate business. Most of us enter the real estate business after spending some years in another field. Although this picture is changing slightly as more colleges and universities start to offer degrees in real estate, generally an office of twenty agents would represent almost that same number of different previous careers. When new agents are able to transfer their previous expertise into helping build their new business, the results can be very positive. We have already suggested that you consider using any previous career contacts as a possible basis for a niche market. They certainly represent a potential source of clients. Take this one step further and seriously evaluate the skills and business techniques that you used in any other business area and see how they might help you develop your new niche marketing business.

Doris spent almost fifteen years of her life before real estate operating a large music studio and teaching in it. There she developed skills in scheduling and preparing classes. Also, she learned how to match up students and teachers who would work well together. And she recognized the importance of staying fully up-to-date on all of the latest materials and information available in her field. She was then able to bring these same skills with her into her new chosen field of real estate.

■ BRANDING YOURSELF

One ideal that all makers of consumer products hope to achieve is that of branding, when you automatically think of one particular brand of a product. For example, when you ask some-

IN REAL LIFE | Mark Nash

Historically in real estate marketing, sales agents focused most of their marketing dollars on advertising their listings to the public. When I started in the real estate sales business, I wanted to follow some recent consumer product marketing strategies. In addition to marketing my listings, I wanted to start branding my real estate sales practices. These practices included sharing with consumers as much information as I had about the transaction process and market, not merely keeping the information. I realized that the consumer had access to as much market inventory and sales information as I did, so I needed to find new benefits and values for me to add to their process. Niche, or target, marketing to specialty or interest-based consumer groups allowed me to focus and build relationships first, and to market my real estate transactions services second. Building relationships first and marketing myself later was contrary to established practices in real estate sales. Most agents want to prospect today, show property tomorrow, and write transactions on the weekend. I wanted a more loyal relationship-based business based on the value that I brought to my clients' transactions.

one for a small piece of tissue to blow your nose, you ask for a Kleenex. When you need a copy of a settlement sheet, you ask the secretary to Xerox it. And when you're thirsty, you might ask your friend for a Coke. Wouldn't you like to be branded as the real estate professional who can best meet the needs of your consumers? Mark Nash brought his expertise from the field of consumer product marketing into real estate as he developed his own branding of his services.

■ NICHE MARKET ACCOLADES

After obtaining your niche clients' permission, always use their positive accolades in marketing to the other members of their niche group. If you are giving seminars or making a presentation to a group, bring along some of your satisfied clients to tell their own story. If you are sending out flyers or a newsletter be sure to include some of those glowing accolades. This reinforcement will help other niche members to remember you and perceive the value of your services when their real estate needs become active. When grateful clients ask what they can do to repay you for your help, ask them to write you a brief letter expressing their satisfaction. Be sure to ask for permission to use it in your personal marketing.

■ NICHE MEMBER RELOCATION

When niche members relocate into a new area, they will most likely have few niche contacts in their new location. Even if you are not able to represent them in the purchase of a property, you can still be a resource for them and assist them as they become networked in their niche. Some of these incoming niche members will need your services later when they want to buy a house. Either way, being a reliable resource provides an additional way for you to develop new clients and referrals. You may even find that your niche can be expanded from a local orientation to a national one.

IN REAL LIFE | Mark Nash

After laying the local market foundation for my niche real estate sale business, I wanted to expand my niche marketing to a national level. I knew from my relocation experience that an affirming niche agent could help transition gay and lesbian transferees into my market. Also, I was receiving phone calls from local gay and lesbian clients or referrals who were looking for an agent in their destination city who was gay, lesbian, or friendly to either. After some research I discovered Crossroads Relocation Referral Network, a national gay and lesbian relocation business run by Jann Henry. Crossroads accepted me as a referring and receiving agent, and I could now help clients moving out of my market to find a niche realtor in their new market.

◼ RELOCATION CLIENTS AS A NICHE

Relocation clients can constitute a niche market in and of itself. We have discussed assisting members of your niche group as they relocate into your area. Another side of this is to specifically work with those who are relocating, developing them as a special niche market. For example, you could become the absolute expert in helping people moving into your own metropolitan area. Anyone moving into a new area needs information on taxes, licensing requirements, utility hookups, school systems, public transportation, and medical and recreational resources. Unless you have made a major move yourself, it is hard to imagine how helpless you can feel when absolutely everything is different.

Some agent might develop a further defined relocation niche in working with people in a specific category such as the military, or a large company like IBM or Mobil. There are many parts of the country with large military facilities. Military wives and retirees, for example, have a ready-made niche in working with their own personal contacts, which soon spreads to others moving either into or out of their area. In Washington, D.C., many people work for Congress—not just representatives or senators, but the multitude of staff people who come along with them. This, too, has become a special niche market for many agents in the D.C. Metro area. A change in the administration is great for business!

ADDITIONAL NICHE MARKET TYPES

We have previously discussed various types of niche markets, in other chapters but here is an expanded list of consumer segments to give you more ideas on selecting a niche.

- Young singles

- Young married/partnered

- Families with young children

- Empty nesters

- Seniors

- Elderly transitional

- Employment based: medical personnel, policemen, firemen, military, flight attendants, etc.

- Gender: working mothers, stay-at-home fathers, single person, head-of-household

- Ethnic/heritage

- Ethnic/immigrants

- Interest: related to hobbies, sports, clubs

- Cultural: related to music, dance, theatre, arts

- Political

- Handicapped: specific health issues, barrier-free housing, breast cancer survivors

- Spiritual/religion

- Members of professional organizations

- Property types: upper-bracket, specific condo/co-op
  buildings, ranch/farm properties, bank or FHA/VA
  foreclosures, teardowns

A recent article in the *Chicago Tribune* described a brokerage
firm that specializes in the teardown market. These are properties that are attractive to a builder solely due to their location.
The builder does not care about the size, age, or condition of
the house since it is to be torn down anyway. The builder just
wants the empty lot in order to construct a new home to meet a
specific purchaser's desires. The seller avoids the inconvenience
of having their home on the market to the public. The new purchaser gets the home of his dreams. In some areas the teardown
market can be quite lucrative.

■ REAFFIRMING THROUGH EVENTS AND ACTIVITIES

Chapter Five discussed building your niche through attending or sponsoring special events or activities for your niche
market. This is very important in the constant reaffirming of
that niche market. Any city or town with a fairly large popula-

IN REAL LIFE | Mark Nash

After several years of supporting the suburban gay and lesbian community, I decided that this niche group could benefit from an event that would bring the community together and through which I could reaffirm my commitment to them. I called several businesses owned by gay, lesbian, or people affirming them and asked for their cosponsorship of an event. They all thought the time was right and committed their sponsorship. Expo 2000 was a hit with the suburban gay and lesbian community. It offered suburban Chicago gays and lesbians an opportunity to meet others in the community and to become acquainted with gay-owned and lesbian-owned suburban businesses, resources, organizations, and entertainers. Over one thousand people attended the event. Media coverage included a Chicago television station, *The Daily Herald* (largest suburban Chicago newspaper), and LesBiGay radio. The success of Expo 2000 reflected all the hard work that went into bridging and supporting the community. The relationships created from this single event still drive a segment of my real estate sales business today.

tion of persons from another country or ethnic group is likely to hold celebrations commemorating a national holiday or special event. If you have selected a particular national or ethnic group as your niche, educate yourself about their special days and see if there is something coming up that you can help with or perhaps sponsor. If not, perhaps you could start one. This "In

Real Life" shares such a special example that reaffirmed commitment to a particular niche group.

■ CONCLUSION

When consumers enter your local real estate market to sell or purchase a home, the home is the product that they are buying or selling. The consumer is motivated to enter the market by the end product, or the home. The bundle of real estate services in the transaction process is what today's real estate professional is actually selling. Our services are the consumer's perceived value of what the real estate sales agent adds to the product purchase. The long-term commitment to establishing solid relationships with those of the niche market community is what makes the difference in how the niche consumer perceives the value of the services provided. The niche marketer is often able to utilize skills learned in a previous career to assist in initial marketing or in strengthening relationships. The niche market develops a special "brand name" for providing superior service to those either entering or leaving the local market. Whatever special niche you have chosen, you must keep this consumer perspective in mind throughout your real estate sales career. Without the consumer being driven by the need to buy or sell property, we have no basis for our business. Remember, the consumer can choose from a variety of service providers or real estate sales agents. Adding value to the transaction for our niche clients is our goal. This will define and build our real estate sales business.

■ STEPS TO NICHE MARKETING SUCCESS

1. Build a presence to your niche by speaking to them publicly at least twice.

2. Be interviewed by the media at least twice as a member of the niche.

3. Build five niche-related business-to-business networks for making referrals.

4. Ask for five to ten niche members' testimonials to use in your niche marketing.

5. Ask for at least ten referrals from niche members.

6. Book seven additional media hits for your niche.

8

Cross-Marketing Beyond Your Niche

Chapter Six talked about the importance of marketing that goes beyond newspaper advertising and monthly mailings. Another part of "marketing beyond" is to extend the relationships you have built with your original core of niche members even further by tapping into each one of the niche members' own sphere of influence, the group of friends and relatives that they know. In this Chapter we will spend some time describing different ways to extend your sphere and why that becomes so important in niche marketing. We will also look at additional spheres that you can work with, such as other agents in your geographic area, local businesses, and providers of other real estate services. There are also people who are not direct members of your selected niche group but who have good contacts with people you have already included on your own sphere-of-influence list. The circles build upon each other, ensuring an ever-growing base of prospective client contacts.

■ YOUR SPHERE OF INFLUENCE

The idea of prospecting by using your sphere of influence may perhaps seem a little too old-fashioned to new marketers, but it still works. This is the one prospecting technique that everyone can afford and that anyone is capable of doing. It costs virtually nothing to make either a phone call or to write a personal note. A personal hand-written note is rare in these days of e-mail, and it would probably come as a pleasant surprise to most people—and quite possibly have a greater effect. The greatest benefit of contacting through e-mail is the speed with which you can reach out to so many people all at once. Even a personal note can still be done much quicker through e-mail than taking the time to hand-write your message. However, think about your goal: is it to establish a relationship or to make what at best may be a lukewarm contact? Because niche marketing is so strongly relationship based, working the sphere of influence makes even more sense now than ever before.

You probably already have a database of current and past clients and other people whom you contact on a regular basis either as a geographical or personal farm. This becomes the starting point. Let this original sphere know that you have developed a new specialty. Encourage them to contact you about people whom they feel you can assist with your new knowledge and expertise. No matter which of the many possibilities you have chosen for your special niche, it is highly probable that members of your original sphere will know people who fit that niche. And even if they never refer anyone to you, it has given you the opportunity to contact them and make them aware that you are constantly expanding your area of expertise in your real estate practice.

IN REAL LIFE | Doris Barrell

Many years ago, I took a real estate marketing course where I was first taught how to develop my sphere of influence. I've never forgotten it, and I've taught it so many times that my friends and colleagues start waving their arms around in a big circle—a sphere—when they see me coming! Let's look at this concept from the viewpoint of the niche marketer.

Statistics indicate that almost everyone knows at least 200 people. Start with these acquaintances as your initial database, making contacts, developing a system for maintaining contacts, and keeping good records of the results of those contacts. Out of the initial 200, how many do you think will want to either sell or purchase property this year? Perhaps only one or two. However, that isn't the point, is it? What you want are the expanded circles that are created by each of your first 200. Even if each of them only has one contact this year whom they refer to you, that adds up to 200 prospects.

Take into account that each one of your original group also knows at least 200 people, each of whom could produce one or two prospects a year, and you start to realize the enormous potential. The spheres keep expanding, and so does your business.

The circles just keep expanding. Your original sphere may now consist of 400, 600, or even 1,000 names. Now your job is to develop a good system for maintaining contact with these people. You must maintain the relationship through regular contact in order for the members of your sphere to think of you when they are considering buying or selling a house. Find the means of maintaining contact that works best for you. It can be by phone, mail, or e-mail; the method is not important. Maintaining regular contact is what counts.

■ BUSINESS-TO-BUSINESS MARKETING

Another effective way to build your real estate sales business is marketing directly via letters and phone calls to housing offices at colleges and universities, corporate human resource offices, and other businesses that have a supply of new people relocating into your market area. Relationships can be built with rental housing businesses that may have clients who have decided they would rather purchase. The trade-off benefit that can be offered back to the rental housing office is to refer to them any buying clients who need to rent at least temporarily before they can purchase a home. Marketing to other real estate transaction service providers, such as attorneys, mortgage brokers, appraisers, and inspectors, is another good source of referrals.

A Note of Caution: The Real Estate Settlement Procedures Act (RESPA) is always concerned about real estate professionals receiving any form of kickback from referral business. You must be careful not to establish any type of financial reward that is to be exchanged in return for referring someone to another service provider. Also, state laws may require that someone must hold a real estate license in order to receive a referral fee based on a real estate transaction.

If you are in an area with a large military population, make sure the appropriate people in the housing office know you by name and are aware of the special services you can offer to incoming families. Many of the different installations have an open house program where real estate agents can come to present their programs. If no such program is offered in your area, be the first to volunteer to give a brief presentation on buying and another on selling. Volunteer to speak at your local chamber of commerce, Rotary club, business executive's club, or other such organization. If you have ever been the person in charge of programs for any organization, you know how hard it is to come up with an interesting and affordable program every month. Keep your talk informational—don't push yourself—and you will not only be asked back, you will probably gain some business. Whatever your niche, there is probably an existing group that meets on a regular basis where you could offer to speak and present your services.

■ AGENT-TO-AGENT MARKETING

Developing a postcard program for quarterly mailings is not a new idea when it comes to contacting your sphere of influence, or in farming. Consider using the same approach to other agents. Sending out regular communication to other real estate agents, whether locally, regionally, or even nationally, is another effective marketing tool. When attending trade seminars, conferences, or relocation programs, take the time to meet and develop relationships with agents outside your market area to build referral business. The next time you attend a meeting, do not sit down next to the people you already know. Select a table full of strangers and tell them about your expertise in your special niche market. Stress that you will promise to give their referral clients your best-quality service, plus a nice referral fee to the agents.

You do not need to wait until you feel you are established. Take time early in developing your real estate business to build a referral database of agents outside your area to whom you can refer clients and who will refer clients to you. The business relationships that you establish with other agents (especially those who share your same niche interests) will provide not only more business for you, but a great source of pleasure. Many will become life-long friends. These additional resource people will bring you market information and customs, stories, and new ideas that you can use in your business. There are many agents today who make their living strictly from outgoing referrals. They no longer work with clients directly. This can be a great source for retirement income.

■ NETWORKING NON-NICHE CLIENTS

Real estate transactions are a vehicle for personalities and relationships to interact. To be a successful part of this transaction, you need to build relationships through networking. Think about all of the relationships you have with many different people and see if there are ways for you to professionally network these relationships. Consider your spouse or partner's professional and personal spheres of influence. Your closed transaction and existing client spheres could contain niche members and potential clients available for your real estate sales business. Social acquaintances, current or past neighbors, service providers to you and your home, board or committee members, your children's contacts, and relatives are all there for you to consider. And do not forget the other people who are often part of the real estate transaction: the painters, plumbers, electricians, carpet and tile layers, landscapers, and house cleaners. In fact, anyone that you come into contact with as a result of assisting a client in the purchase or sale of property is a potential networking source.

■ NICHE TRANSACTIONAL SERVICE PROVIDERS

One of the services we offer our clients is to make the real estate transaction experience as pleasant as possible from con-

IN REAL LIFE | Mark Nash

As my real estate sales business visibility grew, I received many referrals from the gay and lesbian community, and their friends, relatives, and business associates. The cross-marketing was highly beneficial. I received an overwhelming amount of business from people friendly to gays and lesbians. I continued to market to the community and decided to focus on the lesbian community as a subniche. I purchased a real estate business sponsorship and personally became a contributing donor of Mildred's Circle, a health clinic that targets lesbian women. I chose a women's health nonprofit organization because of the many years they contributed resources to fight the AIDS crisis. I felt the give-back was overdue from the men's community. The response from the lesbian community in my support of their efforts propelled me to continue cross-marketing and discovering new subniches.

tract to closing. Be sure to have lists of niche-friendly transaction service providers who are both professional and knowledgeable about the special needs of your niche group. You can assure your clients that they can depend on friendly and sensitive service when they select providers from this list. No one likes last-minute surprises when dealing with a real estate transaction. As you find professional transaction service providers who are a good match for your niche group, stay in close communication with them and let them know that they have been added to your quality-centered list.

■ OVERCOMING THE LANGUAGE BARRIER

Language is one problem that may arise when working with a niche immigrant group. If you have ever been to a settlement where everyone else at the table—the buyers, sellers, cooperating agent, and the attorney—speak the same language but you do not, you know how out of it you felt. Transfer those feelings to how your clients feel when they are confronted with the same situation, except that they are the ones who are out of it. Even though the other agent and the settlement attorney may be from another country and can converse easily with your clients, remember that any real estate professional practicing in the U.S. must also have a good grasp of English. Spend some extra time with such professionals (a good trade-off for their inclusion on your special referral list) and have them explain some of the important real estate phrases from their language. Also, remind them that even though you do not speak that language, you are there to represent your client and it is essential that you be included in the conversations.

Because Hispanics are becoming such an important part of our national demographic picture, consider enrolling in a Spanish class. If you do not have local community college or adult education courses available through your city or county, check out the Internet. Several on-line courses are available. No one will expect you to instantly be able to explain the details of an adjustable rate mortgage or the complexities of title insurance. If you can just learn some of the important terms used in *Bienes Raices* it will help. At the very least, learn enough to be able to greet people, ask about their health, and generally make them feel welcome and comfortable.

With other languages that may not be as accessible for quick learning, form a bond with one of your original members of the niche group and ask them to work with you with members of the group who do not speak English. All too often, we find agents attempting to communicate with a new client through the translation services of the client's eight-year-old child. As heart-warming as this may be, it may not result in an accurate translation.

■ UNDERSTANDING THE AGE BARRIER

Some REALTORS® are also attorneys or CPAs, but most of us are not. This is where we may need extra help when working with the seniors niche. Most seniors have not bought or sold property in many years, and the changes in tax and estate laws are as significant as the changes in the real estate industry. You, as their agent, should certainly be familiar with the Taxpayer Relief Act of '97 and the benefits received when selling a personal residence, but do not try to help them fill out their annual IRS forms. The same is true for the much-discussed estate tax limits. The federal limit may have increased to $1 million per person, but each state has its own estate tax requirements. Bring in the experts; do not run the risk of being accused later of providing false or incorrect information. This is where the team concept can be very beneficial (see Chapter Six).

■ CONCLUSION

A team of real estate service providers who will work with your niche members and make them feel comfortable and knowledgeable throughout the real estate transaction is a valuable service to be able to offer to your clients. These providers are also members of your own business sphere and should be professionals whom you can call on for advice from time to time. Hopefully, they will also refer business to you even as you are referring business to them.

Always be aware that RESPA regulations prohibit the paying of any fee for which there has been no service rendered. Fair housing law prohibits steering of clients in any way that might be construed as discriminatory. Exercise caution in these areas and you will still be able to provide the best in services to your clients even as you expand your own sphere of influence.

STEPS TO NICHE MARKETING SUCCESS

1. Join a real estate relocation referral network related to your niche.

2. Find at least two subniches of your primary niche to cross-market your real estate presence and membership.

3. Locate at least two subniches whose issues get lost in main-niche issues.

4. Compile a list of transaction providers who will work well with your niche.

5. Develop a system for tracking information and maintaining contact with your primary sphere of influence.

6. Develop a system for contacting members of your agent-to-agent, business-to-business, and transaction providers supplementary spheres of influence.

A Final Word

Throughout the book we have stressed the importance and the benefits of niche marketing. We recognize that there will probably be problems and pitfalls in establishing this new element of your real estate practice. The hardest part is waiting for all of your good efforts to achieve your goals. Instead of "location, location, location" we suggest "patience, patience, patience." It will take time. This is not a short-term project. And your existing practice will still need attention.

Developing a niche market does not necessarily mean that you no longer work with prospective buyers or sellers outside of your selected niche. In fact, your outside-the-niche business should also grow as the core niche base grows. Certainly the niche members also have many contacts beyond their own group. Remember, the "everyone knows 200 people" statistic; certainly not all 200 will be in the same unique niche. The best niche marketers report that they still obtain at least 20 to 30 percent of their business from beyond the members of the niche group.

Because developing your niche market takes time and requires patience, it is critical that you spend time up front carefully selecting the right one. Look for where your passion lies. You will be spending a lot of time and energy with this group. Pick one where you will have fun and enjoy the experiences! Check out what is available in your community and find where you can best use your talents and skills to provide service above and beyond the buying and selling of real estate.

The main point is to focus your marketing efforts where you will achieve the best results. Larry Romito, who shared his experience with niche marketing to single moms in Chapter Four, has provided us with this great example of the importance of directed marketing:

"I'm a fly fisherman, and the difference between a fly fisherman who's good and one who's not is what's called 'matching the hatch.' This means studying which insects are hatching at the time because those are the insects that the trout are feeding on. Now, where am I going with this? Well, my brother, who's not a good fisherman, fishes for fish and he doesn't catch much. But a friend of mine, who's an outstanding fisherman, fishes for rainbow trout, brown trout, brook trout, etc. And when he goes fishing for, say, brook trout, he studies exactly what the brook trout are feeding on."

Thanks, Larry, for a perfect illustration of matching the marketing to the desires of the consumer. Provide the niche consumer with the services they both want and need. The niche consumers will then provide you with a steady pipeline of business. The steady pipeline of business will ensure you of financial power—through niche marketing!

Appendix A

FAIR HOUSING LAW IN PRACTICE
by Marcia L. Russell

■ CULTURAL DIVERSITY

The twenty-first century real estate professional must understand and respect cultural diversity in order to deal effectively with persons from different cultures. The National Association of REALTORS® has reported that in recent years the United States has received the largest number of immigrants since the 1930s, and after six years two-thirds of immigrants enter the home-buying market. This represents an excellent opportunity for salespersons to expand their clientele base.

In order to establish the necessary rapport to successfully complete a real estate transaction, the salesperson must understand the existing cultural differences. It is important to ask questions and to learn as much as possible about a particular culture or religion.

The salesperson must also avoid making assumptions, or even worse, stereotyping the consumer based on cultural differences. The fair housing law issue of concern here is steering. One solution might be to have the consumer fill out a Needs and Wants Questionnaire to determine exactly what the consumer wants, while at the same time giving the consumer the opportunity to set any limits that are deemed important. For example, an Asian couple might want the front door to face a certain direction because of a religious belief. Others may express a preference not to have certain numbers present in an address based on Chinese numerology, a system where some numbers are considered lucky and others not, based on how they sound.

Even a small misstep can threaten or even destroy a business relationship with a consumer. For example, some Asian business people have a high reverence for business cards. A real estate agent who writes on the card or puts the card in his back pocket and sits on it, has probably irreparably insulted the individual!

■ STEERING

Upon arriving in this country, it is natural for immigrants to want to become associated with people from their own ethnic group. Therefore, real estate professionals may be asked to identify neighborhoods based on ethnic considerations. Also, buyer's agents might be asked the same question by buyers wishing to limit the housing search based on race. Whether identifying neighborhoods based on race or other protected class factors actually violates the Fair Housing Act's prohibition against steering has been the subject of considerable debate.

Steering is the practice of channeling minority home seekers to designated areas and not permitting them access to all available housing. Steering is not a total refusal to sell or rent, but rather a practice that makes certain housing unavailable.

Courts have held that steering violates the Fair Housing Act's "otherwise make unavailable or deny" provision. HUD regulations give several examples of situations that would be considered steering, including any tactics designed to discourage prospects from inspecting, renting, or buying dwellings.

What about situations when the client states a housing preference based on the race or other protected class factors? The case law is mixed on the issue. In *Zuch v. Hussey*, a Michigan case decided in 1973, the court determined that a salesperson's efforts to influence a customer's housing choice on racial grounds would violate the Fair Housing Act regardless of whether those efforts were undertaken on his own initiative or in response to the buyer's initiative

In *The Village of Bellwood v. Dwividi*, a 1990 7th Circuit case, the court held that the Fair Housing Act does not bar real estate brokers from showing black customers homes in integrated and predominately black neighborhoods and white customers homes in predominately white areas if the reason for such differential treatment is simply an effort to cater to the customer's own racial preferences. According to Robert Schemm, author of *Housing Discrimination Law & Litigation*, "*Dwividi* provides a strong endorsement for an agent's right to respond to customer-initiated racial inquiries." A key issue is who initiates the discussion of race. In his decision, Judge Posner made the distinction between brokers who deliberately try to alter customers' preferences in favor of racial segregation and those brokers who honestly try to serve them.

In 1996, Elizabeth Julian, Assistant Secretary for Fair Housing at HUD, issued two letters to the legal counsel of The Buyer's Agent, located in Germantown, Tennessee, attempting to answer specific questions regarding accommodating a buyer's discriminatory preferences. The resulting HUD opinion created widespread controversy, so much so that on December 3, 1996, HUD rescinded the opinion, which had allowed buyer's agents to show homes in specific neighborhoods if the buyer made the request based on race or other protected class factors. Julian stated, "She sent the wrong message." The position had been strongly opposed by fair housing organizations and the National Association of REALTORS® The NAR staff felt that the original opinion could be seen as steering.

In a training manual, the National Association of REALTORS® recommends "that a buyer's agent include language in his or her buyer's representation agreement indicating a commitment to equal housing opportunity and a statement that the agent has no duty to disclose information regarding race or other protected classes."

What then is the solution regarding situations where clients state a housing preference based on race or other protected class factors? One possibility is to direct the buyer to cultural clubs and organizations who might have access to statistical information regarding racial or ethnic makeup of various neighborhoods. Obtaining the information from a source such as this would not violate the Fair Housing Act. The buyer could then request that the real estate agent show homes in specific neighborhoods that they have identified as potentially meeting their housing needs. If the real estate agent refuses to show the buyer homes in these areas, the agent runs the risk of violating the act by not making all housing available.

In *Hannah v. Sibcy Cline Realtors,* (Ohio Ct. App. 2001) the court was asked to determine whether a real estate agent or a broker has the fiduciary duty to: (1) inform a client whether a neighborhood or community is ethnically diverse, or (2) direct the client to sources to provide ethnic diversity information. The Hannahs wanted a home in an ethnically diverse neighborhood in an excellent school district. The agent informed them she could not give them that information, but did send them school guidebooks. The Hannahs purchased a home in a neighborhood after the principal of the school indicated that the school was ethnically diverse. They then sued the real estate agent when their child turned out to be the only African-American boy in his third grade class.

The trial court ruled that the Hannahs had not demonstrated that a real estate professional had a duty to inform the client whether a neighborhood was ethnically diverse or to direct the client to resources concerning this information. The Appeals Court upheld the decision and further stated that in order to avoid claims of unlawful steering in violation of the Fair Housing Act, it would not be in the best interests of an agent or broker to do so. Imposing such a duty on real estate agents or brokers to give information about the ethnic makeup of a neighborhood would prove detrimental to the goal of fair housing.

■ THE FAIR HOUSING ACT

The Fair Housing Act prohibits the following discriminatory housing practices:

- To refuse to sell or rent after the making of a bona fide offer, or to refuse to negotiate for the sale or rental of, or otherwise make unavailable or deny, a dwelling to any person because of race, color, religion, sex, familial status, or national origin.

- To discriminate against any person in the terms, conditions, or privileges of sale or rental of a dwelling, or in the provision of services or facilities in connection therewith, because of race, color, religion, sex, familial status, or national origin.

- To make, print, or publish, or cause to be made, printed, or published any notice, statement, or advertisement, with respect to the sale or rental of a dwelling, that indicates any preference, limitation, or discrimination based on race, color, religion, sex, handicap, familial status, or national origin, or an intention to make any such preference, limitation, or discrimination.

- To represent to any person because of race, color, religion, sex, handicap, familial status, or national origin that any dwelling is not available for inspection, sale, or rental when such dwelling is in fact so available.

- For profit, to induce or attempt to induce any person to sell or rent any dwelling by representation regarding the entry or prospective entry into the neighborhood of a person or persons of a particular race, color, religion, sex, handicap, familial status, or national origin.

- To discriminate in the sale or rental, or to otherwise make unavailable or deny, a dwelling to any buyer or renter because of a handicap of—

  - that buyer or renter,

  - a person residing in or intending to reside in that dwelling after it is so sold, rented, or made available,

  - or any person associated with that buyer or renter.

- To discriminate against any person in the terms, conditions, or privileges of sale or rental of a dwelling, or in the provision of services or facilities in connection with such dwelling, because of handicap of—

  - that buyer or renter,

  - a person residing in or intending to reside in that dwelling after it is so sold, rented, or made available,

  - or any person associated with that buyer or renter.

- To refuse to permit, at the expense of the handicapped person, reasonable modifications of existing premises occupied or to be occupied by such person if such modifications may be necessary to afford such person full enjoyment of the premises, except that in the case of a rental, the landlord may, where it is reasonable to do so, condition permission for a modification on the renter agreeing to restore the interior of the premises to the condition that existed before the modification, reasonable wear and tear excepted.

- To refuse to make reasonable accommodations in rules, policies, practices, or services, when such accommodations may be necessary to afford a handicapped person equal opportunity to use or enjoy the dwelling.

- To fail to design and construct covered multifamily dwellings for first occupancy after March 12, 1991, that are accessible to and usable by handicapped persons.

- To deny any person access to or membership or participation in any multiple listing service, real estate brokers' organization or other service, organization, or facility relating to the business of selling or renting dwellings, or to discriminate in the terms or conditions of such access, membership, or participation, on account of race, color, religion, sex, handicap, familial status, or national origin.

- For persons whose business includes engaging in residential real estate-related transactions to discriminate against any person in making available such a transaction, or in the terms or conditions of such a transaction, because of race, color, religion, sex, handicap, familial status, or national origin.

■ IMPORTANCE IN PRACTICE

Today's real estate professional must have an in-depth understanding of the Fair Housing Act before attempting to target market a particular group. The Fair Housing Act prohibits discrimination based on race, color, religion, sex, national origin, familial status, or handicap. In addition, state and local laws may also have additional protected classes such as marital status, source of income, and sexual orientation.

The Fair Housing Act prohibits any advertising, notices, or statements that indicate a preference or discrimination based on protected class status. In other words, it is just as illegal to show a preference for a protected group as it is to discriminate. HUD's advertising guidelines specifically condemn advertising that selectively uses media, human models, logos, and locations to indicate an illegal preference or limitation. This includes advertising in particular geographic-coverage editions of major metropolitan newspapers, or in newspapers of limited circulation that are mainly advertising vehicles for reaching a particular segment of the community.

Certain groups are not covered by the federal Fair Housing Act. For example, one's profession is not a protected class. A real estate licensee could target people such as doctors or lawyers without running afoul of the act.

It is also important to note that the Fair Housing Act does not prevent people from marketing their real estate services to any protected group. Thus, a real estate professional seeking to do business with a particular cultural group might consider placing ads in a phone book reaching that segment of the population.

Appendix B

NICHE MARKETING WEB RESOURCES

First-Time Home Buyers
U.S. Department of Housing and Urban Development
www.hud.gov/buying/index.cfm

RE/MAX First-Time Buyers Page
www.remax.com/buyers/firsttime/

Fannie Mae
www.homepath.com

Mortgage.Interest.com
www.interest.com/firsttime/

Children
Federal Children's Sites
www.kids.gov

The Global Schoolhouse
www.globalschoolnet.org/GSH/index.html

PBS did you know?

www.pbskids.org/did_you_know/

Promising Practices in After School

www.afterschool.org/programs.cfm

Scholastic

www.scholastic.com/index.asp

Ethnic Resources

My America Cultural Resources

www.pbs.org/myamerica/honk/resource/cultural.html

Ethnic Resources

www.folkculture.org/links.htm#Ethnic%20&%20Cultural%20Web
%20Links

Ethnic Resources

www.people.geoportals.com/geofolks.asp

Gay and Lesbian

Chicago Gay & Lesbian Networking Association

www.cpna.org

National Gay & Lesbian Chamber of Commerce

www.nglcc.org/benefits.asp

National Gay & Lesbian Law Association

www.nlgla.org

Gay & Lesbian Medical Association

www.glma.org/home

Gay & Lesbian Relocation
www.crossroadsrelocation.org

Immigrants
Immigration and Refugee Services of America
www.refugees.org
www.irsa-uscr.org

Lutheran Immigration and Refugee Service
www.lirs.org

Church World Service
www.churchworldservice.org

The Domestic and Foreign Missionary Society
www.dfms.org

Hebrew Immigrant Aid Society
www.hias.org

People with Disabilities
The Architectural and Transportation Barriers Compliance Board
www.access-board.gov/sec508/508standards.htm

Disability History Museum
www.disabilitymuseum.org

Disability Social History Project
www.disabilityhistory.org

National Accessible Apartment Clearinghouse
www.forrent.com/naac/

Smithsonian Institute's History of Disability Rights Movement
www.americanhistory.si.edu/disabilityrights/welcome.html

Men
Divorced Fathers
www.dadsdivorce.com

Father's World
www.fathersworld.com/mail.html

National Fatherhood Intiative
www.fatherhood.org

Work at Home Dads
www.wahd.com

Professional Organizations
Australia New Zealand American Chamber of Commerce
www.anzaccne.org

Black Career Women
www.bcw.org

National Association of Chambers of Commerce
www.2chambers.com

US Women's Chamber of Commerce
www.uswomenschamber.com

United States Hispanic Chamber of Commerce
www.ushcc.com/HT_show_nov_15.htm

National Association of Women Business Owners
www.nawbo.org

National Society for Hispanic Professionals
www.nshp.org

Professional Organizations in Education
www. library.gmu.edu/resources/edu/edorg.htm

Religion and other Spiritual Resources
All religions represented/Info
www.religioustolerance.org/

Buddhist Information and Education Network
www.buddhanet.net

Digital International Buddhism Organization
www.buddhism.org

Christianity.com
home.christianity.com

Some Large Christian Denominations
Baptist—www.baptist.org
Catholic Online—www.catholic.org
Episcopal—www.ecusa.anglican.org
Lutheran—www.lutheran.org
United Methodist—www.umc.org

Hinduism Online
www.himalayanacademy.com

About Hinduism—What You Need to Know
www. hinduism.about.com/mbody.htm

Al-Islam
www.al-islam.com

Islamic Studies—University of Georgia
www.arches.uga.edu/~godlas/

About Judaism
www.judaism.about.com

Judaism 101
www.jewfaq.org

Seniors
American Association of Retired Persons
www.aarp.org

Senior Corps: Corporation for National & Community Service
www.seniorcorps.org

Seniors' Non-Profit Housing
www.seniorsites.com

Seniors' Information
www.seniors-site.com/referenc/websites.html

Seniors Real Estate Specialist
www.seniorsrealestate.com

Women
www.women.com

International Women's Websites
www.research.umbc.edu/~korenman/wmst/links_intl.html

National Women's Chamber of Commerce
www.thewomenschamber.com

Women in Sports
www.gslis.utexas.edu/~lewisa/womsprt.html

Women's Studies
www.mith2.umd.edu/WomensStudies/

Women's Council of Realtors
www.wcr.org

Police and Firefighter Organizations
Fraternal Order of Police
www.grandlodgefop.org

National Association of Police Organizations
www.napo.org

Firefighting.com—an online community for Fire, Rescue, and
EMS Personnel
www.firefighting.com

American Firefighter.com (with a section for classified ads)
www.american-firefighter.com

Military
Active
National Military Family Association
www.nmfa.org

Military Now.com (with housing and relocation resources)
www.miliarynow.com

See also Professional Organizations

Veterans
U.S. Department of Veterans Affairs
www.va.gov

American Legion
www.legion.org

Veterans of Foreign Wars
www.vfw.org

Community Organizations
Rotary International
www.rotary.org

Kiwanis
www.kiwanisinternational.org

Daughters of the American Revolution
www.dar.org

Big Brothers/Big Sisters
www.bbbsa.org

Lions Clubs International
www.lionsclubs.org

Optimist International
www.optimist.org

YMCA
www.ymca.net

YWCA
www.ywca.org

Rental Property
Institute of Real Estate Management
www.irem.org

Homestore.com—Housing and Renting Resources
www.homestore.com

BuyIncomeProperties.com - An Income Property Resource
www.buyincomeproperties.com

National Association of Residential Property Managers
www.narpm.org

Index